ONE HOUR MARKETING

ONE HOUR
MARKETING

THE ENTREPRENEUR'S GUIDE
TO SIMPLE, EFFECTIVE MARKETING

*Find Your Target Market,
Get More Clients and Build
a Stronger Business Fast!*

HERMAN POOL

New York

ONE HOUR MARKETING
THE ENTREPRENEUR'S GUIDE TO SIMPLE, EFFECTIVE MARKETING
Find Your Target Market, Get More Clients and Build a Stronger Business Fast!

© 2017 **HERMAN POOL**

Published in New York, New York, by Morgan James Publishing. Morgan James and The Entrepreneurial Publisher are trademarks of Morgan James, LLC.
www.MorganJamesPublishing.com

The Morgan James Speakers Group can bring authors to your live event. For more information or to book an event visit The Morgan James Speakers Group at www.TheMorganJamesSpeakersGroup.com.

ISBN 978-1-63047-960-2 paperback
ISBN 978-1-63047-961-9 eBook
ISBN 978-1-63047-962-6 hardcover
Library of Congress Control Number:
2016901311

Shelfie

A **free** eBook edition is available with the purchase of this print book.

CLEARLY PRINT YOUR NAME ABOVE IN UPPER CASE

Instructions to claim your free eBook edition:
1. Download the Shelfie app for Android or iOS
2. Write your name in **UPPER CASE** above
3. Use the Shelfie app to submit a photo
4. Download your eBook to any device

Cover Design by:
Rachel Lopez
www.r2cdesign.com

Interior Design by:
Bonnie Bushman
The Whole Caboodle Graphic Design

In an effort to support local communities, raise awareness and funds, Morgan James Publishing donates a percentage of all book sales for the life of each book to Habitat for Humanity Peninsula and Greater Williamsburg.

Get involved today! Visit
www.MorganJamesBuilds.com

To Anita.
You have made me more than I thought I could be.

CONTENTS

| | Preface | ix |
| Introduction | *The Missing Piece of Marketing* | xi |

Chapter 1	Establish the Right Marketing Mindset	1
Chapter 2	Learn to Set Goals Effectively	16
Chapter 3	Defining Your Target Market	36
Chapter 4	Create Your Message	44
Chapter 5	Know the Tools of Marketing You Can Use	57
Chapter 6	Create a Marketing Sequence	73
Chapter 7	Write Your Marketing Plan	99
Chapter 8	Execute Your Marketing Plan	106
Conclusion:	What's Next?	116

| | Acknowledgments | 118 |
| | About the Author | 121 |

PREFACE

I am so happy and honored you have selected my book. It means a lot to me to have my writing in your very hands this very minute. In the next few chapters, I will share some personal stories of my journey as an entrepreneur who decided to focus on marketing in order to succeed.

When I was young, poor, and struggling I found a few books on marketing in my local library. I did not have the money to afford those books so finding them at the library was a real blessing. The things I learned from those books completely changed my understanding of how to become successful in business.

There is really one skill I have that has best supported me and that is the ability to simplify complex knowledge so I can use it myself or teach it to others. The goal of this book is to provide you with a fast, simple way to embrace and execute a marketing strategy that can give you a clear path to enjoy the type of success my clients and I have had.

I do not have all the answers. I am not a guru. I am just like you. I am someone who wants to improve not only the life of my family, but the lives of my clients, employees, and anyone that doesn't mind doing the work it takes to succeed.

If you are helped by this book or have a question, please visit my website at http://www.hermanpool.com

Thank you and best wishes.

Herman Pool

Introduction

THE MISSING PIECE OF MARKETING

If you've picked up this book, I'm going to go out on a limb here and assume that you need help with marketing. Maybe you're an entrepreneur starting from scratch with a new business. Maybe you're a small business owner whose old (or nonexistent) marketing plan isn't working, or a marketing director looking for a fresh and effective approach. If so, you've come to the right place.

However, I need to be honest with you. Let's say I snapped my fingers and handed you the perfect marketing plan, tailor made for your personality, your business model, and your ideal clients. If you're like most entrepreneurs and business owners I work with, you'd probably say thank you, put it in your to-do pile, and let it get buried under more "urgent" tasks. So many business owners—even when they know they "should" be marketing—find a reason not to. I think it's because, deep down, many people resist the very idea of marketing. I know, because I was one of the many business owners that fell into that camp.

So many business owners—even when they know they "should" be marketing—find a reason not to.

In the mid-90s I was a teenager going to college, working a job at a retail store called Computer City, and living at my parents' house. One day I was helping one of my professors write some lesson plans for a class on computers and he asked me, "Why don't you start your own business? You don't need a degree for that." For some reason, I instantly gravitated to his advice. Maybe a little too much, because I dropped out of school that day and quit my job at Computer City.

I went home that day super excited to tell my mom I was going to start a business. I burst into the house and said, "Hey Mom, I dropped out of school and I'm going to start my own business." To my mother, this news was sudden, it was risky, and it didn't sit well.

My mother gave birth to me when she was fifteen years old and dropped out of school to take care of me. When I was old enough, she went back and got her GED, went to college, and became an educator who specialized in helping at-risk students. In other words, she specialized in helping kids stay in school. She loved me, but she just couldn't support my decision to drop out of college. So, I had the option of returning to school or moving out. I chose to move out.

If you've taken a risk to start a business or follow a big dream, then I know you can relate. The people who love us the most don't like to see us take risks because they don't want to see us get hurt. Nevertheless, sometimes you have to sacrifice to be an entrepreneur. So I sacrificed.

Like so many entrepreneurs before me, I started my first business with a really small budget and a mindset to save as much money as possible so I could invest in my new venture. All I had to my name when I started was a blue Honda Accord and a few hundred dollars. I decided that I would spend money on inventory rather than waste it on rent. During the day, I went door to door in the 100-degree heat of South Texas selling memory upgrades to business owners so I could establish relationships for future business. At night, I slept in the backseat of my little blue 1989 Honda Accord.

I soon found that my Honda was great to get around in but made for a terrible apartment. Not only that but going door to door in South Texas in 100-degree heat in a suit is not the most comfortable way to do things. I had to find a better way.

I felt my services were better than a lot of my competitors. So, why were they getting more work than me?

The Importance of Marketing

I figured out the answer was marketing. All these guys were marketing, and I wasn't. Like many business owners, I just felt that marketing was a waste of time and that word-of-mouth and great service were the only things I needed to have a great business. Yet here I was living in a car, working my rear off every day, and I just wasn't getting enough business to make it all work.

It seemed that the competition knew something I didn't. I needed to know more about marketing. So, I went down to the library and began by looking up the definition of marketing. Here's how Merriam-Webster defines "marketing": "1(a): the act or process of selling or purchasing in a market. 1(b): the process or technique of promoting, selling, and distributing a product or service. 2: an aggregate of functions involved in moving goods from producer to consumer."

Not surprisingly, that didn't help me very much. Luckily I read a number of other books on marketing and eventually I learned that marketing is a science. This was something I could work with. Remember the basic scientific method we learned in elementary school? We begin with a hypothesis (or a theory), we come up with an experiment to test the hypothesis, we run the experiment, and we look at the results. If our results disprove our hypothesis, we come up with either a new hypothesis or a new experiment, and we run it all over again until we consistently get the results we want.

I realized that I had some wrong ideas about marketing, and I needed to change my mindset a little bit. That's when my learning really began. I started exploring other teachers and dozens of other books, I audited college courses, and I ended up in analysis paralysis. I had taken in such a huge amount of information at once that I didn't know what to do next.

Sometimes crisis and overwhelm have a way of forcing us to start over and get back to the basics. So I asked myself, "What are the common denominators between all of these experts and theories? What do Jay Levinson, Philip Kotler, Seth Godin,

Rosser Reeves, and David Ogilvy all have in common?" To my surprise, it was simple. A process began to form in my mind:

1. Establish the right mindset
2. Know how to set goals and execute them effectively
3. Know your target market
4. Know your message
5. Know what marketing tools you can use to communicate your message with your target market
6. Use those tools in the right order, or sequence
7. Dedicate at least one hour a week to marketing.

Once I applied these seven concepts to my marketing plan and put the plan into action, I started to see results. Within 18 months, I saw a 300 percent growth in my business. It's been over 20 years and now making money just isn't an issue for me anymore. I believe the key to that success is marketing.

The Missing Piece: The Marketing Plan

You probably already know a lot of what you need to market your business effectively. However, if you're like most people, you're missing one very important piece: how to put the steps in the right order so they can work together in a system. That's what a marketing plan does. It helps you put all the right pieces in the right order, in order to meet a specific marketing goal.

A marketing plan helps you put all the right pieces in the right order, in order to meet a specific marketing goal.

Over time, with the knowledge I gained from continuing to market my own business, I had the opportunity to open a marketing business to help other business owners achieve the success I did. I began to speak and teach about marketing. Soon I was regularly doing one-hour marketing consults on the phone with entrepreneurs and small business owners.

Here's the problem a lot of my clients would run into. They would run a newspaper ad, run a television ad, or maybe even buy pay-per-click (PPC) advertising, and they wouldn't get the results they wanted. They'd see newspaper ads, television ads, and pay-per-click ads working for other people, and get frustrated and think they were getting ripped off. They were spending the money and doing what they thought they should do: why wasn't it working? They didn't understand that the reason the ads worked for other people was because the other people's ads were part of a plan.

For example, let's say you decided to make an investment in marketing and run a newspaper ad. You call up the newspaper and say, "How much is a half-page ad?" The advertising sales rep says, "A half-page ad is X dollars, but we'll give you a full-page ad for only X more dollars. Larger ads have far more impact." Why does the sales rep suggest a full-page ad? Because he's doing sales. His job is to make money for his company, and he's giving you exactly what you asked for. What he's not doing for you is telling you how that ad is going to contribute to your overall success.

Any individual supplier of advertising and marketing services would tell you their ads work because they do work for some people. What they don't tell you, or possibly what they don't know, is that they only work in combination with other marketing activities, all connected by a plan.

Although there were a few marketing concepts they needed help with, what my clients really needed was a marketing plan to put everything together step by step, so they understood why they were doing what they were doing, and their marketing would have measurable results.

In *One Hour Marketing*, we'll cover the same ground I typically cover with my clients. We'll talk more about how marketing is a science that can generate measurable results, how to set goals effectively, how to identify your target market, how to identify the marketing tools available to you, and how to put them in a sequence. At that point, creating your marketing plan in chapter 7 should take you about one hour or less.

All you have to do is follow the instructions in this book, and you'll be surprised at how easy marketing can be.

If you're looking for a mind-blowing new marketing trick that claims to change the world as we know it, this isn't the book for you. I'm not interested in reinventing the wheel. If you're interested in a simple, proven marketing process that has helped my clients and I grow our businesses many times over, you've come to the right place.

If you're interested in a simple, proven marketing process that has helped my clients and I grow our businesses many times over, you've come to the right place.

Building a business doesn't have to be such a struggle, and neither does marketing. We're all suffering from information overload these days. You just need a clear process and a plan. That's what makes all the difference, and that's what you'll find in this book.

Let's get started by dispelling some common marketing misconceptions to make sure you're starting with the right mindset.

Chapter 1

ESTABLISH THE RIGHT
MARKETING MINDSET

Before we start talking about the importance of mindset, let me give you my definition of marketing: *Marketing is everything you do to communicate your value to others.* Marketing is not a short-term strategic project, or something done randomly or haphazardly whenever you feel like it. Marketing should be a fundamental part of the way you do business every day. Whether you're running new advertisements, coming up with new ways to answer your phone, or just regularly calling your clients to check in with them (which, by the way, is the best marketing of all), you're always going to be marketing.

Marketing is everything you do to
communicate your value to others.

Now that we know what marketing is, let's talk about what it's not. Marketing is not difficult. In fact, it may just be your mindset that's making it difficult. When I first began my business, I had a really hard time getting my mind around how to do marketing right. Ultimately, what I learned is that I had some serious misconceptions about marketing that were getting in the way of my success. These myths came from a variety of places. Some I had been taught and some I picked up on my own, but in order to realize the success I wanted in my business, I had to re-educate myself and get my head right about marketing. It's time to embrace marketing.

Marketing is not difficult. In fact, it may just be your mindset that's making it difficult.

In this chapter, I want to help you overcome the mental challenges that stop you from marketing. Maybe you've tried marketing before and felt its effectiveness just couldn't be tracked. It's possible that negative encounters have made you feel marketing is just a bunch of lies.

Those beliefs are going to keep you hold you back from success because they stop you from marketing—even if you have the perfect marketing plan right in front of you. Whatever your feelings are, I want you to set them aside and understand that there's a reason people market. People market because it *works*—when it's done properly.

So before we talk about how to market properly, let's dispel a few common misconceptions about marketing.

Misconception 1: Marketing Is Manipulation

Not too long ago, I was speaking at a conference in New Orleans about how marketing can help every business grow and succeed. As I'm speaking, I notice a man in the audience shaking his head "no." You get those sometimes, so I press on and don't think too much about it. I finish my presentation and eventually make my way to the reception that followed.

At the reception, the guy approaches me and says, "Hey, you had a great presentation, but you were completely wrong about your definition of marketing."

I always have room to learn, so I say, "Okay. Can you tell me your definition of marketing?"

The man, who stands at about 6'7", puts his arms on my comparatively small 5'11" frame and forcibly pushes me to the side. "That's marketing," he says.

"What do you mean, 'that's marketing'?" I ask, annoyed.

He replies, "Well, let me show you again." He grabs me and forces me to move to the side again. "That's marketing."

"So you think bullying tactics and shoving me in a direction I don't want to go is marketing?"

He says, "No, no, no . . . it's manipulating people into doing what you want."

I reply, "Well, I wouldn't use the word manipulating, and I'll tell you why. The moment you put your hands on me and moved me, I thought, *This guy is a big jerk*. So while I did what you wanted me to do, my impression of you from now on will be *that guy's a big jerk*. Your definition of marketing instantly created a negative reaction in me about you and whatever you want me to do. Now I might let you force me into it once or twice, but I'll never do anything for you again because you've lost my trust and have made me think less of you."

That's it in a nutshell, isn't it? This guy had the idea that he should use his marketing to trick or force people into taking action. We've all been on the receiving end of this type of manipulative, bullying type of "marketing," and modern purchasers want nothing to do with it.

The Truth: Marketing Is Not Manipulation!

Effective marketing never involves manipulation or bullying. Sure, some people use these tactics, but over the long run, people stop trusting the people who use manipulations and look elsewhere. Manipulation is *not* marketing.

Effective marketing never
involves manipulation or bullying.

Misconception 2: Marketing Is Bragging

Another common marketing misconception is believing marketing is bragging. Most of us were taught to be humble and not to brag about our accomplishments. If we played sports as kids, after the game we lined up and said, "Good game," to the other team, whether we won or lost. As we continued collecting achievements in school and then at work, we were taught that we shouldn't be the ones saying how great we are; we should let other people do that.

The Truth: Marketing Is Not Bragging!

However, when we become entrepreneurs and business owners, the rules change drastically. It's still true that it's best when others talk about how great you are, but nobody will know how great you are in the first place *until you tell them yourself.* You have to go first. In the world of the entrepreneur, you have to share the accolades you've received from others because you're the only one who knows them.

Being the first to share the good things others have said about you provides a model for others who also have had positive experiences with you or your company. They'll feel more comfortable telling you and others how positive their experience has been with your company, or how you're particularly good at x, y, or z, when they see others doing it first—giving you more accolades to publicize. As more and more people share positive stories with you, and you continue to publicize those stories through your website or social media or elsewhere, you'll reach a critical mass where everything starts rolling: your message is reaching more and more of your ideal clients, more and more clients and colleagues are telling you that you're doing a good job, they are referring you to their friends and associates, and your business begins to grow. The way you do that is by marketing. It's not bragging; it's simply telling the truth. Don't be afraid to step forward and let the world know who you are and how you can help.

Marketing is not bragging; it's simply telling the truth.
Don't be afraid to step forward and let the world know
who you are and how you can help.

Misconception 3: Marketing Is Ineffective

A third reason we resist marketing is that we simply think it's ineffective. One of the biggest reasons I've heard my clients say they don't market is that they feel it is guesswork that doesn't amount to much. I am here to tell you that is the biggest lie business owners tell themselves. The truth is they are scared to lose money with marketing.

Most small businesses operate on a no-frills budget, and many owners consider marketing something they can't afford or a soft expense. Owners have said to me, "I have to pay the bills. Marketing I can cut." True, marketing is an expense that can be reduced or cut. The question that then arises is how, without marketing, do you propose to gain those much-needed clients that mean sales? It's cliché to say you have to spend money to make money, but it is sometimes true. If you do not effectively market your company, brand, image, and products or services, you won't be in business for long.

If your marketing hasn't been effective, it might be because you haven't been taught a methodology that yields repeatable, measurable results.

The Truth: Marketing Is a Science!

I have some great news for you. Marketing is *not* guesswork, and you can indeed measure your results. As long as you treat marketing as a science.

The science that is most closely related to marketing is psychology. Psychologists have spent a long time studying human behavior, and from this data they have mapped out quite well how we make decisions, learn, and take action.

Psychological studies indicate that all purchase decisions occur first in the subconscious mind and are driven primarily by emotion. No matter how much we want to believe that our logical, conscious mind makes the decision, as much as 95 percent of all purchase decisions are made in the subconscious mind.[1]

This understanding is key because it gives us an advantage. Now that we know our subconscious mind makes purchasing decisions, we only have to find a way to speak directly to it. Fortunately, psychologists tell us that the best way to get a message through to the subconscious mind is *frequency* and *repetition*.

Remember, we're talking about effective communication, not manipulation. I'm assuming you're in business because you believe your product or service will truly help people. There are plenty of "marketing experts" who may not have your prospective clients' best interest at heart that are already using this understanding to their advantage. Don't your prospects deserve to hear about your products and services in a way that ensures they can take action?

---

1   That 95 percent of purchase decisions are made in the subconscious or unconscious mind is now common knowledge in the fields of psychology, marketing, and the emerging field of neuromarketing. See Gerald Zaltman, *How Customers Think: Essential Insights into the Mind of the Market* (Harvard Business School Press, 2003); Roger Dooley, *Brainfluence: 100 Ways to Persuade and Convince Consumers with Neuromarketing* (Wiley, 2011), 1; Dan Ariely, *Predictably Irrational* (Harper Perennial, 2010); and Martin Lindstrom, *Buyology: Truth and Lies About Why We Buy* (Crown, 2010).

The Importance of Frequency

In the marketing world, the number of times a person must be exposed to an advertising message before a response is made is known as *effective frequency*. In his article "The Impact of Television Advertising: Learning without Involvement," Herbert E. Krugman explains that psychologically there are three levels of exposure: curiosity, recognition, and decision.[2]

Exposure #1 causes a "What is it?" type of response. Krugman states, "Anything new or novel no matter how uninteresting on second exposure has to elicit some response the first time."

Exposure #2 causes a "What of it?" response. At this point, prospects decide if the product has any importance to them. If they find it does have importance, they are more apt to take action with future exposures.

Exposure #3 is what Krugman describes as "the true reminder." Psychologically, Krugman believes that all future exposures are really just Exposure #3. It's the point at which prospects take action if they were interested as a result of Exposure #2. Krugman felt that people put a marketing message out of their minds until it has some use, which is when the response to the message occurs.

The benefit of these repeated exposures is that the prospect doesn't have to go over all the cognitive steps again. By Exposure #3, they know if they want the product and take action.

---

2   Herbert E. Krugman, "The Impact of Television Advertising: Learning without Involvement," *The Public Opinion Quarterly* 29, no. 3 (Autumn 1965), pp. 349-356.

Remember, Krugman assumes a psychological response for each exposure. Based on that theory, three exposures may be enough for your prospect to make a purchasing decision. However, that doesn't mean you can get away with three ads and it rarely works as easily as this.

Jay Conrad Levinson, the author of *Guerrilla Marketing*, would point out in his presentations that people are inundated with marketing messages today—so much so that your message is missed two out of every three times. Taking into account Krugman's three-exposure theory, your message would have to be seen at least nine times before you'd have any hope of your prospect's action. Even then, the prospect would have to be in buying mode at that sixth exposure to take action. Chances are it will take more exposures than that to find them at their point of need and for them to take action.

Based on what we now know, it isn't unreasonable to think that it will take dozens of exposures before action is taken upon your marketing message.

While there are several thoughts on the number of times a message has to be seen, there is no disagreement about the fact that frequency is key to successful marketing.

The Importance of Consistency

Further, based on Krugman's studies, we know the message delivered should be *consistent*—in other words, it should use the same words. If the message is the same, the prospect will not have to think "What is it?" or "What of it?" again.

A great example of this concept occurred in my first business. I had been saving up my pennies and dollars in order to buy a full-page ad in my local newspaper. As soon as I got enough money to run the ad, I called them and had it run once. It was all I could afford.

I can still remember getting that newspaper with the big ad and running around the shop like a madman shouting, "The newspaper is here! The newspaper is here! I'm somebody now"—just like Steve Martin in my favorite comedy movie, *The Jerk*. I was quite proud of making enough money to advertise my business. It was a significant amount of money. I honestly felt that this ad would change my fortune.

Unfortunately, after weeks of no significant business increase from that ad, I learned the hard lesson that one-off ads don't generally work that well. Sure, sometimes you can hit a home run, but it doesn't happen every day. I realized that this large ad just wasted money that took me a decent amount of time to make.

I decided it had to be the copy, so I rewrote the ad, saved up, and ran a new one a month later. When that didn't work, I ran another two months later with different copy. By my third time, I felt like a moron.

I looked at all three ads side by side in the newspapers to figure out what I did wrong. That's when I noticed another ad that said, "Run your business-card-sized ad for $40/wk." I was spending 40 times that on the large ads.

I called the newspaper and ordered the smaller ad. This time, I ran it every week and left the copy the same on each run. What I put in that ad was really simple. It was just a picture of a lady screaming with the "Home Alone" face, looking at her laptop, and all it said was "Don't worry, we can fix it," with a phone number and nothing else.

For the first month, nothing much happened.

The second month we saw a slight increase in sales.

On the third month, something happened. The phones rang frequently every day and we saw nearly a 200 percent increase in sales.

Frequency and consistency pay off. When done right, marketing works wonders.

Frequency and consistency pay off.
When done right, marketing works wonders.

The Importance of Measurement

Now some of you may be wondering, how could we be sure it was the newspaper ad that made that 200 percent difference? Because we thought like scientists running an experiment. We had a way to measure our results. We listed a special tracked phone number in the ad so we could measure the response rate for that ad alone. If someone called in on that phone line, we knew they had seen the ad. We always used tracked phone numbers in our ads, and we ran unique phone numbers in each phone book we advertised in. Apparently we were also unique in measuring our results.

We discovered this about a year later when the sales representative from the phone book company paid us a visit. He told us, "It's time to write a new ad. This year our phone book is going to be smaller, but lucky you, you only need to pay 10 percent more than last year."

I said, "Man, that sounds like a great deal. Ten percent more for a smaller ad—you're a good salesman." (If you haven't noticed yet, I have a pretty sarcastic sense of humor.)

I led him over to one of the desks we have up front and spun the monitor around so he could see. "Why don't you sit down here at this desk, and we'll see how your phone book is doing?"

"What?" he said.

"We track the number we run in your ad so we know how many phone calls we get from your book," I answered matter of factly. I pull the number up in our CRM records and it showed fifteen phone calls a month.

I said, "Hmm . . . fifteen phone calls a month. What do I pay you?" He told me what I paid him, which was way too much for fifteen phone calls a month.

"Gee, man," I said, "looks like we've got a problem here. Only fifteen phone calls a week—I guess we just need to cancel."

"Whoa, let me call my boss," he said and walked outside.

He came back in and said, "Listen, we'll give you twice as many ads for the same price."

I said, "Dude—only fifteen phone calls a week?"

"All right," he said, and he walked outside again.

This time, he came back in and said, "We're going to give you twice as many ads at a lower price than you paid last year."

"That's a deal," I said.

Not long afterward, the sales rep from another phone book came in. I said to myself, *Boy, I've got this down pat.* I invited him to sit down.

"Hey, let's talk about your ad," he said.

"Let me guess," I said. "Ten percent more."

"No, sorry—30 percent more."

"Well, that's great. Let me guess: smaller phone book."

"Oh, much smaller. We took out the residential section so nobody is going to read it," he answered. (Okay, he didn't really say that, but it was true.)

"Fantastic," I said. "So, 30 percent . . . let's sit down and look at this." I pull up his phone number and I show him the report. "What's this?" he asked.

"We track the phone number we run in your ad so we know how many calls we've gotten."

"Really?"

"Yeah, it also tracks into our CRM, so we know how many sales we have off these phone calls. So let's look." I looked at the screen, and it said twenty-five calls per week.

I looked at him and said, "We're only getting twenty-five phone calls a week from you. That's not good enough." So he walked outside, came back in, and said, "Hey man, we'll give you two times the ads at half of the price."

"You win," I said. "I guess I'll take that deal, and we'll see how you do next year."

Neither of the sales reps had any idea what a normal response rate was because nobody had ever tracked them and told them the results.

A lot of people believe nobody uses the Yellow Pages. Since we track our ads, we actually know whether they do or not. I ran that business in a little town, with 10,000 people within the city limits and about 40,000 in the entire area, and we have seven different IT service providers in the area. The previous year they were all in the phone book that was only giving us fifteen calls a week. This year, when the phone book came out, it had my ad and no one else's. Everybody else had pulled out of the phone book.

Just the first week that phone book hit the ground, we ended up with an extra $3500 in sales. The lesson is: Don't assume people aren't looking at a specific advertising medium such as the Yellow Pages. Find out for yourself by testing and tracking the results. Call tracking is an excellent way to test results for all sorts of ad media.

Here are some more examples of measurement tools you can use to track the effectiveness of a particular marketing approach.

Newspaper. When you see "bring in this flyer," "mention this ad," or even "bring in our competitor's ad" for a special deal, those companies aren't just being nice. They're tracking where their advertising dollars are going.

Television. The same is true for those special offer codes mentioned on commercials or infomercials, especially on channels like QVC.

Website. Website analytics (such as google.com/analytics) tell you where your traffic is coming from. If you don't know where your traffic is coming from, then you don't know how to get more traffic there. You could also create different landing pages for certain online or offline ads to track their effectiveness.

E-mail. This is just an electronic version of the paper ads. Companies might ask you to show the e-mailed ad on your smartphone, or scan a QR code.

I hope viewing marketing as a science brings you some sense of relief. Just remember that marketing is never done perfectly the first time. When I first started out, I would get so nervous about doing it exactly right that sometimes I just wouldn't run an ad. With experience, I learned that I was putting way too much pressure on myself. You're not supposed to know what works before you try it – that's what experiments are for!

You're not supposed to know what works
before you try it—that's what experiments are for!

All you have to do is try something, see if it works, and if it doesn't, modify it. You're not going to be perfect every time. Some things will not work as well as others, and that isn't a problem. By testing, measuring results, making small changes, and trying again you can easily fine tune your marketing approach.

The bottom line is that the science of marketing takes frequency, consistency, and measurement. It also takes the ability to set and achieve goals—which is the subject of the next chapter.

The bottom line is that the science of marketing
takes frequency, consistency, and measurement.

Chapter 2

LEARN TO SET GOALS EFFECTIVELY

N ow that you understand marketing is a science, the next step is to learn how to set goals effectively. Whenever I ask clients what their marketing goals are, more often than not I discover that they have never learned how to effectively set and execute goals. Goal setting is a crucial skill for entrepreneurs to master if you want to be successful—not just in marketing, but in any endeavor.

One of the biggest mistakes I ever made in business was not realizing the importance of setting goals sooner. Sure, I read lots of books just like this one that told me how important setting a goal is, but I always just thought it was garbage, motivational fluff. I figured that if I just told myself, "Get more clients," that would be enough to get going. I was so wrong.

Like many of you, there was a point in my life where the economy had taken a toll on my business and my family. Life has a funny way of forcing you to learn sometimes. While working to "get more clients," I met a woman named Anita, eight months later I proposed, four months later we were married, and three months after we were married she was diagnosed with stage 4 breast cancer. It was her second bout with a stage 4 cancer; she had an unrelated cancer five years prior and successfully fought it. This second bout with another cancer made her and her medical team fear for the worst, but they came up with a plan to help her survive. We had to make plans of our own.

We lived three hours away from MD Anderson Cancer Center, one of the nation's top cancer treatment facilities. Their plan was to have us drive up every other week for cancer treatment. My plan was to take as much time off work as possible so I could spend time with my wife.

We made another plan. We weren't sure how long we would have together. I knew there were a lot of things Anita and I wanted to do together, so we decided that running up our credit to do these things was okay. If she lost her battle with cancer, Anita would have done all she wanted to do and insurance could pay off the debt. If she didn't, no big deal. The cards had pretty low-interest rates and we both made enough money to pay off the debt in a few years without impacting our quality of life.

For a few months, it worked out great. My staff handled the day-to-day operations of my business. My wife and I drove back and forth to cancer treatment. I was able to go to every single appointment and treatment day. I took a few weeks off during her hospitalizations and stayed with her at the hospital. When she was feeling good, we would travel to wherever she wanted and do whatever events she thought would be fun.

Two years later, she was clear of cancer. We also had accumulated over $150,000 in debt from medical bills and credit cards. Not a problem, since the business was doing well, right? Well, it would have been fine, except for the fact that in the first year of treatment the credit card industry started losing its mind and raising everyone's rates to the sky. Also, since I had placed myself in the position of salesperson and neglected to put anyone else in that position during this time, my business was staying level and not growing. I was paying an average credit card rate of 9 percent when we received the diagnosis. Now I was paying an average of 24 percent.

Combine all this with my wife not working for eighteen months during the treatment (as I begged her to; she wanted to work forever), and we have a pretty severe problem. What we thought we could pay down comfortably in a few years became a monster that consumed the majority of my funds to pay down in the same amount of time.

Early one morning, a noise like rushing water woke me up. It was a really weird noise to me because it sounded like water running in the house. I checked all the faucets and found them all off, but the noise just kept going. That's when I figured it must be raining. I went to look out the window and found the source.

Water was pouring down the *inside* of my window frame. There was a hole in my roof and water was running down inside my house. I called around for a roofer and found a reasonable quote of $4000 to fix the roof.

With all the credit card pay downs and medical expenses, we had no reserves. All of my cards were maxed out and I was paying several thousand dollars a month just to maintain a maxed-out balance. Things were bad.

The stress of dealing with the finances, my wife's health, my business struggling under the debt load I had created, and the beginning of my own health crisis was beating me down each day. I had to do something.

I knew I needed $4000 to fix the roof. That doesn't sound like a lot to some, but in that crisis mode it was killing me.

So, I wrote "$4000" on a piece of paper. Next to that I wrote, "to fix the roof." I also knew I needed $4000 in 30 days because the roof had to be fixed as soon as possible. So I added "in 30 days" after "to fix the roof." Then I began to assess the different services I sold at my business that could get me $4000 in profit quickly.

I used some simple math to identify how many of each product I would have to sell to hit my goal. Then I identified which services were most likely to get me the $4000 fastest.

That notepad looked something like this:

$4000 to fix the roof in 30 days
What can I sell to make $4000?
Service 1 $20
Service 2 $50
Service 3 $100
Service 4 $200
Service 5 $1500
How many of these sales will it take?

$4000/$20   200
$4000/$50   80
$4000/$100   40
$4000/$200   20
$4000/$1500   2.6

Which services are both easy to sell and can get me where I want to be in 30 days?

Service 4 $200
Service 5 $1500

Obviously, these weren't 100-percent-profit products, but the cost of goods was low enough that I could afford to take that hit better than I could afford to go without a roof.

It seems stupid, even now as I write this all out, but this one simple exercise got my mind off all the pain, mess, and distraction that kept me from dealing with things in a rational manner. It also helped me clarify what I should focus on personally and what my staff should focus on.

My goal was: **I will earn $4000 to fix the roof by selling 5 Service 4s and 2 Service 5s in 30 days.**

Writing down such a simple goal gave me the focus I needed to come out of what seemed like a two-year self-induced zombie state that kept me safe from the reality of life, but also kept me from growing my business to take care of my family.

In essence, that was my marketing goal. From here I decided to create a marketing plan to push these two services. These were newer services we had added in the middle of dealing with cancer, and I hadn't promoted them as much as I should have.

I didn't have much money to spare, so the marketing tools I needed to use had to be as near to free as possible.

Service 4 was a monthly service we sold to business owners to monitor and maintain their servers. I had never really pushed this service much because I was usually out selling higher-ticket services. However, I realized that this product could just as easily be sold by my staff as an upsell to business owners whom we did service for. My staff were not salespeople; they viewed sales as an evil art. They were good at explaining why a client should choose to have work done, though. (Silly technicians. That's sales.) Rather than position them as salespeople, I decided the best thing I could do was educate them on how this service both made life easier on the techs and helped save the clients money. So I wrote on the notepad:

Goal: Sell 20 Service 4 accounts within the next month.

How: Have staff offer this service to every business client we service. Provide staff with a list of benefits of this service and help them understand how it benefits them and the client. Call business owners with servers and less than 10 workstations to offer them a special on their system.

Service 5 was a monthly service designed to help a business owner with ten or more computer systems keep his systems running smoothly and keep system downtime to the absolute minimum. I knew that if I could get seven sit-down appointments with decision makers, I could probably sell two or three accounts. So I wrote this on the notepad:

Goal: Get appointments with 7 decision makers who have more than 10 computers in their office.

How: Generate a list of current clients with more than 10 computers. Call them to make an appointment.

I know that kind of planning doesn't look like much, but in the end, I sold one new $1500/month account with an additional $1500 setup fee, and my staff sold four $200/month accounts in 30 days. Sure, I missed my goal by a couple hundred dollars, but I had made enough to call it a victory.

Beyond the victory of getting a new roof, since I had decided to focus on services with a monthly recurring fee, I actually added $27,600 to my annual income.

My wife was free of cancer, our leaky roof was fixed, and my business was back on track. I knelt down, praised God, and knew I could run my business again.

That made me realize how easy it would be to take down $100,000 in debt. Using the same method, I successfully destroyed that debt within eighteen months. That's a story for another time.

Why Goal Setting Works

Now that I've shared with you how goal setting has been so beneficial for my life and business, let's talk about how goal setting can help you and what it takes to set goals the right way.

Every time I set out to "get more clients," something "more important" would come along and I would get lost and couldn't figure out what I needed to do to return down the path to my goal. Worse yet, "more clients" was so unspecific,

I had no idea when I reached my goal, or in the event I knew I had reached my goal, I had no idea how I got there to repeat the results.

Goals and systems allow you to measure success and repeat the results. Having no system in place for creating, tracking, and measuring my goals was killing me and my business with wasted time and resources. Once I embraced a system for goal setting as an activity that needed to be done, I found myself becoming much more successful in much less time.

Setting goals is a critical part of getting what you want, whether it's in your personal life or in business. There is quite simply no better way to create genuine lasting change. A close look at any achievement in your life will reveal that it was probably not possible without a clear goal and a well-executed plan supporting it. Here are some reasons why setting goals is so essential.

Setting goals is a critical part of getting what you want, whether it's in your personal life or in business. There is quite simply no better way to create genuine lasting change.

Goals Create Clarity

You can only achieve clarity of vision through goal setting. Many of us have vaguely defined desires on our minds, but if there is no concrete outline of what you want, in the end, you'll only be spinning your wheels with no forward progress. Goals must be set twice—once vaguely in your mind, and again concretely in reality. The clearer the goal is in your mind, the easier it is to create solid steps that will get you where you want to go.

Goals must be set twice—once vaguely in
your mind, and again concretely in reality.

Goals Give You Responsibility

Once you have determined your goal and start working towards
it, you create a sense of responsibility. Whether or not you
achieve your goal is solely dependent on your actions and
attitude and has little to do with outside influences. The time
for blaming others for your failure to achieve is over. You are the
only one accountable for your success.

Goals Guide Action

A well-set goal paves the way for a concrete action plan. Simply
wishing for things does not make them happen. You know,
deep down, that today is the best day to start taking small steps
toward your target. An essential part of the process of setting
your goal is breaking it up into mini-goals with a daily plan of
action. (We'll talk in more detail about creating mini-goals and
action steps later in this chapter, and when we get to executing
your marketing plan in chapter 8.) Following the plan means
each day will bring you that much closer to your goal.

Simply wishing for things does not make them
happen. You know, deep down, that today is the best
day to start taking small steps toward your target.

Goals Provide Motivation

How will you know if you have gone off the path without
clear goals? Making progress each day toward your goal by

using your action plan will give you the motivation you need to keep you on target. Tracking your progress allows you to see how far you've come and how much of a shame it would be to let all that effort go to waste. For many, the simple act of putting the goal into words and taking the first tiny steps provides all the motivation they need to see their goal through to completion.

Goals Will Help Keep You Focused

Having goals, and the action plans for achieving them keeps your focus on what you need to do to finally get what you want. Without goals and an action plan, it's very easy to get distracted and lose focus, and you aren't likely to ever achieve those great things you want in life. Setting goals allows you to keep focused on what's most important and shows you where to put your energy each day.

Goals Make Achievement Easier

It's important to set goals, but you must also have systems in place to help you achieve them. Like anything in life, you will need to learn and practice the best ways to set goals in order to master the skill. You're smart and motivated (that's why you bought this book), and there are a lot of changes you can't wait to make in your life and in your business, but you must slow down. Once you've set and met your first goal, you can think about adding the next. Most of us are at risk of burning out if we tackle more than one goal at a time. Besides, life is also about enjoying the path that leads us to our goals.

> Most of us are at risk of burning out if we tackle more than one goal at a time. Besides, life is also about enjoying the path that leads us to our goals.

Don't Reinvent the Wheel: Learn to Set SMART Goals

Setting goals the right way will help you accomplish almost anything, but that doesn't mean it's easy. It takes a lot of planning and action to achieve goals, and many of us simply aren't "planners." Thankfully, the SMART method of goal setting is a way for anyone to set realistic goals that lead the way to success. SMART is an acronym you can use as a guide to set your goals. For a goal to be considered SMART, it is:

- Specific
- Measurable
- Actionable
- Realistic
- Time Bound

Several marketing gurus have recently claimed the idea of SMART goals is outdated and boring and have presented some new process or acronym that's supposed to be newer and better. (Some of them are actually quite clever.) However, my reaction is: "What are you doing? You're mocking this wonderful, simple process of steps and checklists that have helped people actually do what they want to do so that no one will want to use something that actually works, just so they'll buy your products and services." Yeah, steps and checklists aren't super cool, but when you have them, they help you get things done, and when you have money at the end of it, you think, "Hmm, maybe that checklist was kind of okay." Which is what my discovery was.

Yes, the SMART method has been around for a long time, but I've found no better way to set goals effectively. The trick is that although many people have heard of it very few are actually using it.

The SMART method has been around for a long time, but I've found no better way to set goals effectively. The trick is that although many people have heard of it, very few are actually using it.

By the way, not every goal is necessarily going to be a SMART goal. There are really two kinds of goals: long-term goals, which are your overall, overreaching life goals, and then the short-term goals you set to reach those larger goals. Your long-term goals may be more like values or dreams, such as starting your own business, finding work-life balance, or being a good parent. To actually meet those long-term goals, you need to break them down into specific short-term goals, which need to be SMART goals.

You can create as many levels of short-term goals (or mini-goals) as you need in order to reach your long-term goal. Maybe your goal is already clear enough to be an action step, or maybe it's a particularly big goal that needs to be broken down further. Think of a Russian nesting doll: you keep opening each doll until you get to the smallest one in the center. When you set your short-term goal, you keep breaking it down further and further until you can't break it down anymore, and you have a clear action step you can take right now.

If you don't like the doll analogy, here's another one: In football, they use a goal line to measure the big short-term goal: 100 yards from one end of the field to the other.

It takes a lot of steps to get to that 100-yard line. So they break it down into many different downs. Every play that's made in the game is to meet that overall short-term goal of reaching that hundred-yard line. While sometimes there may be an amazing play and the team scores a touchdown instantly, most of the time it's step by step.

(Just so we're clear, I don't know anything about football. I was thinking about electronic football the entire time I was writing that example. So please don't ask me who my team is— I'd be embarrassed.)

Now we'll describe each element of the SMART method, so you can make sure all your short-term goals are SMART goals.

Specific

You're much more likely to accomplish a specific goal than a vaguely defined abstract goal. If you are specific when setting your goal, you can focus on exactly what you need to do to reach it.

Begin by crafting a simple statement that will explain what you want to do. It's important to use the phrase "I will." For my roof example above, my statement would be, "I will earn $4000 to fix the roof."

Next, answer for yourself the "what," "how," and "why" of this goal to break it down further. Try to be as detailed as possible. This process will help you to generate the steps and mini-goals you will need to reach before finally achieving the end goal. I already have the "what" in my statement above, but if I wanted to make my goal more specific, I need to add the "how" and "why."

The "how" was a little vague at first—I knew I was going to earn the money by selling certain products and services, but I had to think about exactly which ones. (We'll get to that in the Actionable section, although some of these descriptors can overlap.)

The "why" was, well, to keep a roof over our heads. At a deeper emotional level, though, it was also about proving my worth as a provider for my family. So here's the new, more specific version:

> *I will earn $4000 to fix the roof by selling the products and services that will get me the most profit the fastest, so I can provide well for my family.*

The "why" is particularly important. As you motor through your list of tasks, it's easy to forget why you started your journey in the first place. Before you begin, have an honest conversation with yourself about the true reasons behind your desire to achieve this goal. Remembering these reasons is an important part of keeping up your inspiration and momentum, and will help keep you on track when things don't go as planned.

If you are having a hard time determining why you'd want to achieve a goal, simply visualize yourself in the future enjoying the product of your work. Picture yourself completing the steps it will take to reach the goal, and then imagine what life will be like after you've achieved it. This in itself may be the answer you are looking for, and will help you answer any other questions that follow.

Measurable

To achieve objectives, you must be able to clearly observe your progress. You must be able to measure your results. The $4000 was already a clear, measurable figure, so I had that covered. By making your goals measurable, you can easily see the progress you are making, which helps you keep your momentum and stay motivated.

Actionable

Specific and measurable goals are great. However, if you don't take action, they are impossible to attain. To make sure your goal is both actionable and attainable, it is best to break down your goals into mini-goals. Once you have your mini-goals, write down the detailed actions you should take to reach them. Consider all the things you could be doing today to bring you closer to your goal.

I made sure my goal was actionable when I figured exactly what services I would sell: I listed all the services I could sell at a profit quickly, and then calculated how many of each service would get me the most money the fastest.

Here's my goal now:

I will earn $4000 to fix the roof by selling 5 Service 4s and 2 Service 5s, so I can provide well for my family.

It's also important to write down action steps to take if things are not going as you had hoped. If the results you're getting aren't what you want, change something, but don't give up.

Realistic

At the risk of being redundant, an unrealistic goal is impossible to reach. Making a realistic goal means you can see the big picture, and you know what you need to do to reach it. You must ask yourself if your goal is something you can do or even something you want to do. Stop and think about your weaknesses and strengths. Which parts of your goal will be difficult, and which will be easy for you? Create a plan that takes the challenges you are likely to face into consideration.

Here I made sure my goal was realistic by creating mini-goals and action steps to reach those mini-goals. I was going to sell 20 Service 4 accounts within the next month, and I planned out exactly how I intended to do that. Then I planned to set up 7 appointments with the appropriate decision makers to sell at least one or two Service 5 accounts.

Time Based

Anyone who wants to reach a goal should outline a timeline for when the main goal and mini-goals should be reached. Mine was a pretty short-term goal, but it was high stress, so writing out a timeline for my mini-goals and action steps was important to keep me focused.

So here's my full SMART goal: *I will earn $4000 to fix the roof by selling 5 Service 4s and 2 Service 5s in 30 days, so I can provide well for my family.*

Many find that reaching a goal takes longer than planned. Even if your timing doesn't match your plan, the urgency created by a timeline will help move you along. Goals you've never achieved before can be difficult to outline; just take a good guess. You can modify your time frame as needed.

How to Measure Progress to Stay on Track with Your Goals

You've set your goal and you're well on your way to achieving it, but how do you know how far you've come? One of the most important parts of achieving your goal is measuring your progress along the way. (That's the point of making your goal measurable.) Keeping track of your progress will allow you to celebrate the successful completion of each step of your goal, continuously recharging your motivation. It also can be a powerful evaluation tool to help you change course if you need to. Here are a few excellent ways to measure your progress.

Figures and Facts

For every type of goal, there is a way to numerically measure it. Some goals that already involve numbers like losing weight or saving money are easy to quantify. For those that aren't, like being a better parent, friend, or manager, you must be creative about finding what you can measure. Being a better parent, for example, could be measured in the hours you spend with your children. A good record of progress toward this goal could be, "I spent 15 hours this week with my kids."

Keeping a Schedule

Those with large goals should create an action plan, which breaks down your goals into smaller steps and sets a timeline for the completion of each one. Keeping up with the schedule you set forth in your plan will help you stay organized and makes it easy to chart your progress. (You'll set up your specific marketing schedule in chapter 8.) It's important to assess whether you're hitting your targets on schedule or not, but you must also know when to be flexible. Keep in mind that the point of creating a timeline is to help monitor progress, and it can be changed at any time.

Use a Journal

Journaling can be one of the most effective ways of monitoring any goal. Every setback and success will be there for you to reflect on, providing a valuable assessment tool. Just open a notebook to the first page and write down the specifics of your action plan in your new goal journal. Try to set aside a few minutes each day to write about your progress. Some like to write letters to their future selves, and some prefer to make lists of random thoughts. Write in whichever way feels right to you. Entries do not need to be long or detailed, but they can be.

Ticking and Tallying

If journal writing isn't exactly your style, you'll probably prefer keeping a simple *tick sheet*. A tick sheet is a list of tasks needing completion that allows you to simply check them off as you go. Go online to download a printable tick sheet, use a calendar, or simply grab a piece of paper and make your own list. If you have the technology available, you can even get free checklist apps for your smartphone or desktop. Each time you tick the checkbox, you are celebrating a success. Your collection of marks will provide a great visual to show you how far you've come toward your goal.

Rankings and Ratings

For the most difficult goals to quantify, creating your own *rating system* will make monitoring your progress much easier. One great way to quantify something is to create a system that goes from 1 to 5, with 5 being the highest. Use that system to rate your progress toward your goal each day with a number.

If you want to be more confident, for example, you can assign a value to how confident you feel at the end of each day based on your rating system. A 5 means you're ready to take on the world, and a 1 means you want to get back into bed and hide. As your daily ratings pile up, you will be able to step back and see the progress you've made and will also be able to see where you've had trouble so you can reflect on how to improve.

You already have so much on your plate and adding one more task to your busy day may seem daunting. Your goal may seem far away, and your daily tasks may distract you from your progress. Every day you set your goal aside, it becomes more difficult to reach. That's why it's worth it to take a little time each day to measure your progress, bringing your goal back to where it belongs at the forefront of your attention. There is a system of measuring goal progress to fit every lifestyle, and the key is finding the one that's right for you.

Chapter 3

DEFINING YOUR TARGET MARKET

A target market is defined as a specific group of consumers at which a product or service is aimed. Many entrepreneurs are so focused on growing their business and so convinced of how valuable their idea is, that they think everyone is their prospective client. This is never the case. Let me illustrate this with a little story.

Goldilocks and the Three Target Markets

One day, Goldilocks decided she needed more clients for her porridge store. At first, she thought, "EVERYONE loves porridge! My target market is EVERYONE, so I need to broadcast an ad to EVERYONE in the nation. I'll buy an ad for the big game! Then EVERYONE will be talking about my store!"

She called the TV ad people and asked, "How much for time on the big game?"

The big game ad exec said, "Only $2.5 million for a 30-second spot. What will you be selling?"

Goldilocks replied, "I sell porridge at my porridge store."

The ad exec smiled and said, "I'm not a big fan of porridge, but I am sure you will do fine. How many spots do you want?"

So Goldilocks realized that not everyone liked porridge and said, "This Target Market is too broad! Broadcasting to EVERYONE is too expensive."

Goldilocks began to think a little more carefully about her target market. Now she thought, "Maybe I should only focus on people who like porridge. Instead of broadcasting to everyone I find, I will send a targeted mailing to my new target market: EVERYONE WHO LIKES PORRIDGE."

As luck would have it, she found a mailing-list broker who had porridge consumer data. She asked the broker to sell her all the names on the list.

The list had 100,000 names and cost 50 cents per name. At $50,000, Goldilocks didn't have the budget to buy the list and mail out her offer.

"This target audience is too large," said Goldilocks.

"Okay. Who usually buys porridge from you?" the list broker asked.

"Most the people who buy from me are mothers," replied Goldilocks.

"What ages are they?"

"Well, they are from 35 to 55."

"Why do they buy from you?"

"Many of them are afraid of how chemicals in store-bought porridge will affect their children. My porridge is 100-percent organic and gluten free."

"Do you think they would travel further than 20 miles for your porridge?"

"No, but I also sell my porridge online through my website."

Goldilocks thought for a minute, and then it hit her. "So my target market is really WOMEN AGED 35 to 55 WHO ARE LOOKING FOR ORGANIC, GLUTEN-FREE PRODUCTS FOR THEIR CHILDREN TO SAFELY ENJOY!"

The broker said, "Well, that brings the list down to 10,000, so it will be far more affordable. Also, we run a magazine called *Porridge Aficionado*. I think your message about organic porridge for busy moms will be very effective in our magazine. Nanocasting to such a specific audience will save you lots of money and increase your conversion rate."

With that, Goldilocks said, "This target audience is just right!"

And she marketed happily ever after.

Finding a Target Market That's "Just Right"

Just like Goldilocks had to, I want you to distrust your first attempt at defining your target market. It is almost never defined or specific enough to be effective. Notice that Goldilocks wasn't able to get specific about her target market until the broker asked her a few pointed questions. By the time Goldilocks was finished, she was able to define her target market in terms of age, gender, parental status, core concern, and geographic area—and her target market was just right.

> I want you to distrust your first attempt at
> defining your target market. It is almost never
> defined or specific enough to be effective.

Taking the time to define your target market in very specific terms provides you several immediate benefits. First of all, it saves you money. Big media like TV, newspapers, radio, and large pay-per-clicks campaigns are tremendously expensive. Trying to reach an overly broad and poorly defined audience with broadcasting is a waste of money. In contrast, a well-defined target market will open up the opportunity of *nanocasting*. Nanocasting simply means communicating your message to as targeted an audience as possible. Opportunities to nanocast are everywhere, but you can't see them until you start looking through the lens of your target market. Nanocasting is not only far more affordable than broadcasting; for most small businesses it is far more effective as well.

> Nanocasting is not only far more affordable than broadcasting;
> for most small businesses it is far more effective as well.

For Goldilocks, broadcasting meant buying a TV ad for the big game for $2.5 million, and nanocasting meant buying a clearly defined segment of a mailing list for $5,000, as well as running ads in an affordable niche publication.

The second immediate benefit is that it gives you the message for your marketing materials. Without a well-defined market, you can spend hours trying to figure out what to say and how to say it. Part of the process of defining your target market is discovering your audience's core concerns, the problems they face, and how your product or service addresses those core concerns or solves those problems. This is called your *unique selling proposition* (USP).

When Goldilocks realized that her audience had a core concern about the chemicals in store-bought porridge and that hers was all natural and gluten free, she discovered her USP. She is not going to have to spend a lot of time wondering what to say in her ad in *Porridge Aficionado*—she just needs to speak to her audience's core concern and explain how her product addresses it. (We'll talk more about creating your USP in the next chapter.)

Five Questions to Define Your Target Market

I hope by now that you're starting to think about *your* target market. Here are the five questions that I use to help clients to define their target market as specifically as possible.

1. Name your target market.

Name your target market, but as I said before, be suspicious of your first answer. It is rarely specific enough to be effective. Your answer here may take several iterations and some creative thinking. I know Goldilocks got it in three tries, but in the real world, it may take more.

Let's use a practical example. Let's say John is the owner of an IT services company. Originally he would have defined his target market as anyone with a computer—but now he knows he's got to do better than that. However, on further reflection, he realizes that the solutions he has to offer really only make sense at a certain scale, so his target market becomes companies with five or more PCs. He could go further with this question alone, but the next questions will push him more quickly to the heart of the matter.

2. Who is the decision maker?

Who makes the buying decision? Whose name is on the credit card? John is able to define his target market further by changing "companies" to "business owners." So his new target market is business owners with five or more PCs. Better, but he could still define it even more.

3. What are your target market's motivators?

What would motivate your target market to buy your product or service? What problems do they have? What emotions are behind those problems? How will people feel after they have purchased your product or service? Remember, people make buying decisions with their emotions, as we learned back in chapter 1. So this step will require *research* and *empathy*. Research will help you discover their problems. Empathy will help you put yourself in their shoes and know what it feels like to have their problems. Internet research, focus groups, and surveys are all tools at your disposal. You can also interview past clients and ask them, "Why did you buy my product or service?"

John, the owner of our IT services company, does a little market research. He finds out the entire medical profession is particularly concerned with patient data security in light of the patient confidentiality laws known as HIPAA (Health Insurance Portability and Accountability Act). It's a constant headache to stay compliant, and if they're found noncompliant, they could face heavy fines that could cause them to lose their businesses.

This provides an opportunity for IT companies like his to step in and help solve the technological problems associated with remaining HIPAA compliant in an increasingly complex virtual world. He learns about the software doctors' offices have to use and the problems with that software. So he decides to offer solutions to the problems that are driving doctors' offices crazy.

The only problem is that every other IT company in his area is doing the same thing. Doctors are already inundated with marketing materials offering to help.

A little more research on his part revealed that companies that sold durable medical equipment, like oxygen tanks, wheelchairs, and walkers, were subject to the same HIPAA compliance requirements, and they weren't inundated with marketing materials like doctors' offices were. So his target market became owners of durable medical equipment companies with five or more computers.

4. How far would they (or you) travel to deliver or obtain service?
Some companies are impacted by the physical distance between their office and their prospects, while others, like online-only businesses, are not. So if you're a brick-and-mortar company, this is a question you need to answer. Don't miss the significance of this step. Goldilocks would have wasted millions of dollars on an ad during the big game, reaching hundreds of thousands of people who could not practically buy from her. I know it sounds far-fetched, but it happens all the time on a smaller

scale. People buy radio ads that cover the entire metro area of a major city when they realistically only serve the west side of the city, inside the beltway. If you happen to have a service where you travel to your clients, such a mistake can result in time-consuming leads where you simply disappoint people by telling them you don't go that far.

John had a physical office, and he needed to travel to his clients' physical offices in order to deliver his services. He knew he was willing to drive 100 miles to do the work at this point. Now his target market was owners of durable medical equipment companies with five or more computers within 100 miles of his office.

5. Where would you be most likely to find your target market?

Once you have a target market that is well defined, a little research, observation, and critical thinking will yield various places you might find your target market. Once you know where to find them, you can figure out how to reach them.

John discovered that only 50 businesses met his description within a 100-mile radius, and their mailing addresses were easy to find. So he decided to nanocast with a direct-mail campaign. Instead of spending a fortune direct-mailing thousands of doctors' offices who would never read his marketing materials, he focused his time and money on the 50 businesses that needed what he had to offer but were largely ignored by the IT companies of his area.

Chapter 4

CREATE
YOUR MESSAGE

N ow that you understand that your target market's buying decisions are driven primarily by emotion (chapter 1) and who your target market is (chapter 3), creating your message is easy. What you want to do is clearly establish how your product or service helps people overcome a problem that they're having and how they feel before and after that problem is solved. That problem might be something very specific and time sensitive, such as "I'm hungry and I want to eat." It might be, "I want to have more free time for my family." Or it might be something as broad as "I want to be successful and make life more fulfilling." Every problem, no matter what it is, has an emotion attached to it. Likewise, the solution to that problem—ideally supplied by your product or service—also has an emotion attached to it. So you want to identify those emotions early on.

The biggest problem entrepreneurs have when trying to create their message is that they believe the features of their service are their selling point. However, features don't sell anything. People don't buy a new computer because it has a fast processor; they buy a new computer because it makes their work go more quickly. They don't buy a car because it's got a V-8 engine; they buy it because they want to go fast. They don't go to the dentist to fill a hole; they go to stop the pain from the cavity. What motivates a client to buy are the benefits. These are the good things that will happen because of the features.

The benefits directly connect our products and services to our clients' emotions. When your message contains the right benefits, your products or services will almost sell themselves.

What motivates a client to buy are the benefits. These are the good things that will happen because of the features. When your message contains the right benefits, your products or services will almost sell themselves.

One evening I was having dinner at a friend's house, and I was talking with a mutual acquaintance who owns a software company about some of his frustrations with an upcoming product launch. "I've got this piece of software that launches on January 1," he said, "but I need a new website—the guys that were doing our website have done a really poor job. I've got to get it done in thirty days. I just know I'm going to contact another web development company that's going to drag their feet and do the same thing to me because I've had this problem before."

At this point, I said, "One of my businesses happens to be a web development company that specializes in helping companies have a better online presence in 30 days or less. We know a lot of people view web developers as flaky and unreliable, so we've developed a solid process to get your website finished in a very reasonable amount of time so you are free to handle the more important parts of your project."

Then it wasn't even a conversation. He just said, "Okay, how much is it?"

I had no intention of selling anything that night—it just happened. Why did it happen so easily? First, I had my target audience sitting in front of me. Second, I knew his problem and the emotions associated with it: he needed a website done in thirty days, and based on his past experience, he felt web developers were unreliable. Third, I told him how the benefits of my particular service would provide an outcome that directly solved his problem—resulting in a positive emotion and the decision to buy.

All I had to say was that we specialized in solving his exact problem. It was that simple.

Another name for this kind of targeted message is your *unique selling proposition* (USP). The concept of the USP was created by advertising executive Rosser Reeves, author of a book called *Reality in Advertising*, in the 1960s. He felt that slick or entertaining copy wasn't enough and that every ad should include a USP. He is quoted as saying, "No, sir, I'm not saying that charming, witty, and warm copy won't sell. I'm just saying I've seen thousands of charming, witty campaigns that didn't sell."

One of the most enduring USPs he created was for M&Ms: "Melts in your mouth, not in your hand." This one well-written statement lasted for decades.

Most business owners lack the power of a targeted USP. Statistics show that most businesses fail. I don't think that is mere coincidence. The USP is a tool you need.

Here's the process I use with my own clients to help them create their USP.

Step One. Start by listing all the *features* of your product or service.

Step Two. Now, in a single list, write down all the benefits of each of these features that are relevant to the target market you defined in chapter 3. If you're having trouble figuring out what benefits your product or service offers to your target market, consider the following questions:

- What is the *desired outcome* of your target market, when they're searching for your kind of product?
- What is the *problem* or obstacle that stops them from having a successful outcome? What gets in the way?
- How does your product or service help them reach their desired outcome? That answer is the *benefit*.

Step Three. Eliminate any benefit on the list that isn't unique to you. After all, other people can help your target market reach their desired outcome, but what is it that sets your service apart? What makes your company different from other companies, what makes your service special, what do you offer that your competition doesn't?

Step Four. Then answer the following questions:

1. What is your most unique benefit?
2. What problem does it solve?
3. How does that problem make the client feel?
4. How will the client feel after the problem is solved?

Now insert your answers in the following blanks to create your USP:

We help __[target market]__ who want ___[1]___ to solve their problem with___[2]__ so they can ____[4]_____ .

Let's return to our IT services company, whose target market is owners of durable medical equipment companies with five or more computers within 100 miles of its office. What might its USP look like?

John, the business owner, went through the process of listing all the features and benefits of his service he wanted to market, which was backup and disaster recovery. He crossed out all the benefits that other companies provided just as well as he did. Then he answered the following four questions. Because he had done the work of defining his target market very specifically, keeping in mind their motivators as we discussed in chapter 3, answering these questions was relatively easy.

1. What is your most unique benefit? [helping owners of durable medical companies stay up to date with HIPAA compliance]
2. What problem does it solve? [possibility of data loss or breach]
3. How does that problem make the client feel? [scared, worried that noncompliance fees could cause them to lose their business]
4. How will the client feel after the problem is solved? [relieved, secure, have peace of mind]

Now he could insert these answers into the fill-in-the-blank USP statement:

We help owners of durable medical equipment companies who want to stay HIPAA compliant solve the problem of accidental data loss or security breach, so they can experience security and peace of mind.

He could certainly do some work to smooth out the language of the statement so it flows more naturally, but he now has a clear message that will speak powerfully to his particular target market.

How to Use Your USP in Your Marketing

So once you have a USP, what do you do with it? Your USP is the DNA of your marketing message, and you can use it in a number of ways.

Create a Tagline

You can create a tagline from your USP. On his website, John might put under his company name, "Providing health care security for durable medical equipment companies."

Create an Elevator Pitch

You can also use your USP as the basis for your elevator pitch. If you don't know what an elevator pitch is, it's a little 30-second speech about your business that you can tell somebody in the time it takes to get to their floor on the elevator. Although it may be tempting to use your USP as your elevator pitch just as it is, you can create a deeper elevator pitch by including your *business identity.*

Your business identity is a description of your roles, values, goals, and characteristics as an entrepreneur or organization. It explains why you do what you do, it establishes the source of your authority, and it's a large part of your brand.

Why is it important to incorporate your business identity into your elevator pitch? Because we know that people make buying decisions made based on emotion, we also know that people do business with people they like. As was famously stated, corporations are people, too. So people don't just do business with people they like; they do business with brands and companies they like.

People don't just do business with people they like; they do business with brands and companies they like.

As you begin to think about your own business identity, think about the kind of terms you'd use to describe the identity of people you know. Perhaps your mother is generous, strict, and organized. Your closest friend may be outgoing, fun, and careless about time. If your organization was a person, how would people describe you? What are your values, goals, strengths, and weaknesses? Create a short list of single-word descriptors, and you've got a pretty good representation of your business identity.

So a compelling elevator pitch should reflect the identity of your business, who you help, how you help them, and the results they can expect when doing business with you—in a short, friendly way.

For example, when thinking about his values and the source of his authority as a business, John writes down the words "20-year army veteran, technical understanding, professional, friendly, detail oriented."

So his elevator pitch might be, "My business helps owners of durable medical equipment companies stay HIPAA compliant by protecting them from accidental data loss or security breaches, so they can experience peace of mind. As a twenty-year Army veteran, security is very important to me, so we do whatever it takes to make sure patient data stays safe."

Collect Client Testimonials

You can also use your USP as a template for clients to give you their own powerful testimonials in the form of a story. When you're looking for your referrals and client testimonials, simply ask your clients: "Did I provide this benefit for you? Did I solve this problem for you? How did you feel afterward?" Once you have those answers, you can craft a powerful client testimonial or client success stories (see the next section for more about client success stories).

Based on its answers to the USP questions above, our IT services company might ask its clients, "Did we help you feel confident you were staying HIPAA compliant? Did we solve your problem of worrying about data loss or security breaches? How did you feel afterward?"

These are just a few examples of how your USP can provide the basis for virtually any version of your marketing message.

The Power of Storytelling

That said, I can't have a chapter on creating your message and not talk about the power of storytelling.

You don't have to think back too far to realize the enormous power of storytelling. Just think back to your own childhood. I know that as a child I loved to have my parents read or tell me a story. Some of my favorite stories were in the form of fables. Fables have a great way of teaching lessons that have formed much of my morality and have even influenced how I run my businesses today. One of my favorite fables is the story of "The Miller, His Son, and the Donkey."

> *A Man and his son were once going with their Donkey to sell him at market. As they were walking along beside the Donkey, a countryman passed them and said: "You fools, what good is a Donkey but to ride on?"*

This caused the Man to be embarrassed. In order to rectify this, the Man put the Boy on the Donkey and they went on their way. Soon, they passed a group of men, one of whom said: "Look at that lazy kid; he rides while his father walks."

This caused more embarrassment to the Man. So, the Man ordered his Boy to get off, and he got on himself. However, they didn't go far before they passed two women, and one said to the other: "Shame on you, you lazy jerk. Making your poor boy run alongside you."

"What to do?" thought the Man. Now, he picked his Boy up and they sat together on the Donkey. They had finally reached the town, and the passers-by began to jeer and point at them. The Man stopped and asked, "What are you complaining about?" The men said:

"Aren't you ashamed of yourself for overloading that poor donkey with your heavy frame and your heavy son?"

The Man and Boy got off the Donkey and tried to figure out what to do. They thought and they thought until the Man had a solution. The Man cut down a branch to use as a pole, tied the donkey's feet together, ran the pole between its legs, and carried the Donkey upside on their shoulders. They continued along through the laughter of all who met them till they came to the Market Bridge. As they crossed, one of the Donkey's feet got loose. The Donkey kicked out and caused the Boy to drop his end of the pole. In the struggle, the Donkey fell over the bridge, and as his other feet were still tied together, the Donkey drowned.

Moral of the Fable: Try to please all, and you will please none.

I know this story has helped me through problems as an entrepreneur, and I am sure it is a lesson that we can all learn from. The bigger lesson here is that this powerful story has been passed down for centuries, as have many others because we seem to be hardwired to respond to storytelling.

Psychologists Melanie Green and Tim Brock have delved deep into what they call "transportation into narrative world," which they say is "a type of mental involvement that may facilitate the integration of knowledge from the narrative world into real-world judgments."[3] To put it more simply, people will put themselves in the position of a character in the story and make real-world decisions based on the impact of the story. If you can take your product or service message and integrate it into a story, then you have a winning combination.

Allstate's "Mayhem" campaign is a great example of storytelling in modern marketing. The campaign features a character named Mayhem who causes trouble while telling you the story about how much pain that trouble is going to cause you. By this time you can identify with the poor person who is a victim of Mayhem, it's at this point that Mayhem adds something to the effect of, "Should have called Allstate, they would take care of this mess and make it good as new." At the time of this writing, the Mayhem character Facebook page has

---

3   "Melanie C. Green," Social Psychology Network, http://green. socialpsychology.org. Also see M.C. Green and T.C. Brock, "The Role of Transportation in the Persuasiveness of Public Narratives," *Journal of Personality and Social Psychology* 79, no. 5 (2000), 701-721.

around 1.6 million fans and was ranked by Facebook to be in its top five brands globally.

One great way to use the power of storytelling in your marketing is to share your message in the form of a story. For instance, John's IT services company could fashion stories around themes like how their product saved Joe's business when a hard drive died unexpectedly, or how Nancy was able to keep her data secure after a major storm.

The really nice thing about thinking in these terms is that it can lead you to think of actual events where your product has helped someone, which can become a client success story. When you do find an actual event, don't just make it a bunch of facts. Tell readers about what happened in story format. Remember to include these basic elements when writing your client success story:

- **Introduction:** Set up your introduction to allow readers to identify and feel close to your story's characters. Draw on common emotional needs of your target prospects.
- **The problem:** Delve deep into the problems the character faces and the emotional struggles the character feels. This allows the reader to put themselves into the narrative world.
- **The solution:** Just as your character is dealing with the harsh problem, your company or product can be presented as a hero to save the day.
- **The resolution:** Be descriptive about the positive emotion your characters feel once the day is saved. As

we learned in chapter 1, people are often best motivated to buy based on the feeling they get after they use a product or service.

Chapter 5

KNOW THE TOOLS
OF MARKETING
YOU CAN USE

Now that you have your message, you need to communicate it to your target audience. Historically, this process of communicating has been called *advertising*. Advertising has always been an important part of marketing, but thanks to the advancements of the Internet, changes in advertising have been huge. As a result, most people talk about marketing (communication) tools in terms of different types: offline, online, outbound, and inbound. Just in case you're not familiar with these types, let's review them briefly.

Offline Marketing

In the Beginning There Was Print

Once upon a time, local and regional newspaper publishers controlled the way that small companies advertise. For many decades newspaper and other *print* publishers had the final say in how business owners got their company's message out. They had the expensive printing presses, they had the staff of writers to keep people's interest, and most importantly, they had the audience.

Business owners understood that if they wanted their message seen by others, they had to pay the print publishers to get noticed. The problem was that newspapers and other print media only had so much room for ads, so if a larger competitor could spend more it had a great advantage over a smaller company.

Along Came Radio

Radio became another form of advertising that small businesses could utilize. Radio reached a large audience and had the power of voice to help make a marketing message even more powerful. Like print, radio had a limited inventory, so larger companies soon became the ones that really benefited from radio ads because they had the capital for multiple ads that saturated the market.

If a Picture Is Worth a Thousand Words, What Is Video Worth?

Later came *television* advertising. This was a great new way to reach thousands of people right in their homes. However, the downside to having your ad placed on television was the enormous cost for a single sixty-second commercial. Only large national companies could afford TV time, thus pushing out smaller local businesses. Since companies with large budgets bought up prime viewing times, one of the ways small businesses saved money on television ads was to run their commercial very late at night when few people were watching.

Online Marketing

The birth of the Internet has changed marketing for the better. Now businesses of any size can choose what size of audience they want to reach and for a fraction of the price. In fact, a tech-savvy small business owner can start an ad campaign on the Internet for almost nothing at all but time. This has given small companies around the world a chance to compete on a national and global level with companies many times larger than them. This leveling of the playing field is just what small business owners needed to get the word out about their products and services. Now for little to no money, ads generated by small companies are seen by millions of people each day.

A tech-savvy small business owner can start an ad campaign on the Internet for almost nothing at all but time. This has given small companies around the world a chance to compete on a national and global level with companies many times larger than them.

For example, when *social media* became popular, it gave small businesses the chance to reach smaller, more focused groups of people. Many of these groups were actively seeking what small companies were offering. An example is a group of cat lovers who get together online and discuss all of the wonderful aspects of owning a feline. This target group would be perfect for a small startup cat-food company trying to break into the market.

Blogs are another form of cheap advertising that small businesses can utilize. When a company builds a blog and starts to attract readers, a brand is formed. This powerful online brand is a small company's voice among the masses. Having your own brand will allow you and your product or service to be recognized around the world. This is a great way to attract new clients from around the globe, which will help your bottom line. Many blogs have become viral and have even become profitable all on their own. When other companies see you have the attention of a high percentage of their target market, you can charge other companies to place ads on your blog, which can provide even more money flowing into your small business.

Social media is another great tool for small companies that can attract tons of followers who can, in turn, become loyal clients. Keeping up with your clients and letting them know about all the exciting new products your company has to offer is easy with free social media sites such as Facebook, Twitter, LinkedIn, Instagram, and more. A simple short message or picture will help clients keep you in mind when it comes time to make purchases.

Internet forums are also a great way to spread the word about your small business. Forums allow you to focus your advertising on people who are already interested in what you are offering.

Say you are a company that grinds its own form of specialty coffee. A great place to advertise your product would be a forum that caters to coffee lovers. With the wide range of different forums out there, you are sure to find one that fits your business model. If by chance you can't find a forum that fits your needs, why not create one? This will give you 100 percent control over how your branding is placed, and best of all, it won't cost you a dime.

No small business would be complete without having a *website* of its very own. Just like having a blog, a website can help you build your brand. Not only can you advertise your brick-and-mortar business, a website also allows you to break into the world of Internet e-commerce. This is a great way to increase sales, and the possibilities are endless when it comes to the number of clients you can reach. Having a website set up and maintained can be more costly than running a blog or using Twitter, but it will give you complete control over your brand and how you wish to present yourself to the world.

A great way to get the most out of all of these online opportunities is to connect each one. By linking your website to your blog and forum, all that blog and forum traffic can flow straight to your website. Also, by linking your social media accounts such as Facebook, Twitter, Instagram, and others to your website, you can stay in touch with all of your clients with one click of the mouse.

As with anything else, it's tempting to think that newer is always better, and many people believe online marketing tools are inherently better than offline. However, just because there are new ways to market doesn't mean the old ways should be completely abandoned. At my company, we still use the Yellow Pages, newspaper ads, and direct mail and I have my most successful clients do the same. The modern difference is that now we combine them with things like our website, social media channels, and e-mail marketing, to get our message seen many times across multiple media channels.

Outbound Marketing

Outbound marketing is an approach to marketing that has to do with initiating communication with existing or potential clients. It can include both offline and online marketing tools, such as e-mail, direct mail, cold calls, print ads, and out-of-home advertising. The benefit of outbound marketing is that it tends to create an opportunity for an immediate response or reaction from clients.

Due to its direct nature, many companies still utilize outbound marketing strategies heavily within their overall marketing mix. Outbound marketing usually has measurable results that are proportionate to the time and effort spent by those executing it, which is why it is still very popular with established businesses. Recent advancements and techniques, like tracking numbers, have allowed even traditional print media such as direct mail to be tracked and qualified regarding their ability to generate online leads and conversions.

E-Mail Marketing

E-mail is the most widely used form of communication today. E-mail is accessible at any time from any location and nearly any device today, making it an extremely effective marketing platform. Unlike calls or online advertising, e-mail is not an "interruption" media, allowing clients to engage with it at their convenience.

E-mail marketing tools, such as MailChimp, Constant Contact, and my own e-mail marketing tool AxionMail, allow not only for mass e-mail marketing but a way of tracking and verifying the effectiveness of your e-mail campaigns to clients. The success metrics associated with e-mail marketing include open rate, bounce rate, click rate, and unsubscribe rate.

Ideally, e-mail marketing can be used to gain new clients; however, it is also an effective way of maintaining a relationship with your existing clients. By using an e-mail newsletter to keep them up to date with important information, major changes within the industry, or the services you will be providing them, you can keep clients engaged and feeling like you are receptive to their needs.

Direct Mail

Many marketers believe print is dead, but that is not strictly true. Print can be leveraged as a gateway media to drive traffic to your website and gives you an opportunity to make an impact with tangible media. *Direct mail* can still be an effective marketing tool because it creates a sense of personalization that digital media often fails to do. Providing some type of value, such as a discount or directing them to a special online message such as video content or a free download, is an effective way of transitioning clients from your print materials to engaging with your brand online. One of the complaints about print media is the difficulty in tracking its performance and conversion rates.

This can be overcome by utilizing specialized URLs and QR codes and tying them to your analytics. This will allow you to track the performance of print material much the same way you would an online banner campaign.

Cold Calling

Cold calling is one of the cornerstones of traditional outbound marketing. It is also one of the forms of outbound marketing that are more difficult to make efficient. Cold calls are usually reduced to being a numbers game, but effective cold calling has more of a strategy behind it than this and can be essential to conversions for your business.

Another important aspect of cold calling is to make sure that your employees are utilizing some type of Customer Relationship Management (CRM) system. This allows them to document important information from their interactions with clients so that other employees who contact them in the future have all the information they need to meet the clients' needs or close a sale.

Print Ads and Out-of-Home Advertising

Print advertising is still relevant to many industries and is a major part of the branding effort of any business. *Print and out-of-home advertising*, such as billboards, allow companies to communicate their presence and offerings to clients in a broad way, without a client necessarily having the ability to shut them out. Direct mail ads can be thrown away, e-mails can be detailed, phone calls can be screened, but display advertising such as billboards and bus signs are harder to ignore.

While a good marketing mix will take advantage of both inbound and outbound marketing strategies, outbound marketing and its effectiveness often relies heavily on the sales force executing it. The effectiveness of these campaigns is determined by the level of commitment of your team members and their ability to utilize effective communication skills. Outbound marketing also allows you to dictate the narrative and present your products and services to your audience in a way that best suits the situation and the market.

Inbound Marketing

By contrast, inbound marketing is a long-term strategy that may have a longer turnaround time for lead generation or conversions. However, inbound marketing is an extremely important method of marketing you should be using today. Any good marketing mix should utilize both inbound and outbound marketing strategies; however, there are some specific benefits to inbound marketing.

Some of the unique benefits of inbound marketing for businesses include the ability to automate many of the tasks associated with it, and the fact that it is a very powerful long-term marketing strategy for lead generation, conversions, and increasing overall website traffic and brand awareness.

Various methods of inbound marketing include social media, search engine ads, press releases, content marketing, online display advertising, and search engine optimization. These methods all have different advantages and goals associated with them. Additionally, despite the fact that much of this marketing involves "one to many" communication, it often feels more personalized to users who are interacting with it, because they are making a decision to do so in most cases.

Social Media

Social media is probably the most popular and well-known method of inbound marketing. Social media allows you to publish information about your brand to a wide audience while also giving them the opportunity to share it with others. Social media is essentially the twenty-first century's version of word of mouth.

Social media platforms that businesses usually are able to effectively use to connect with their audience are Facebook, Twitter, Instagram, LinkedIn, and YouTube. These sites have the highest overall levels of engagement and the largest audiences. LinkedIn is a great place to post articles that share valuable information about your industry and establish your credibility. Facebook, by contrast, is usually used to more directly connect with clients and can be used to help provide customer service, support, and feedback, and keep clients informed of changes or other things they may need to know.

Twitter is ideal for sharing resources with your audience, such as free downloads and links to articles your company has published that may be helpful. It can also be used as a listening tool to stay current in real time about trends and important events related to your industry or client base.

YouTube is a great way to put a face to your brand that users can identify with. YouTube is considered the second-largest search engine in the world, and the level of engagement it offers is staggering. YouTube can be used by companies not only to distribute commercial advertisements but demonstrate their products and services and make potential clients aware of what they have to offer.

Search Advertising

Paid search engine advertising is a good inbound marketing tactic because it allows you to specifically target users who have an interest in your product services. You will often see this referred to as pay per click or PPC. Search engines, like Google, allow paying advertisers to use a number of criteria for determining who sees their advertisements and under what conditions. These criteria include scheduling times, limiting ads to locations, and controlling which search terms trigger advertisements and what page they direct to.

As a result, search advertising is one of the most effective inbound marketing methods and has easy-to-follow success metrics to determine ROI, since it utilizes tracking and conversion codes, showing which specific campaigns and ads are resulting in conversions/sales or generating leads.

The argument can be made that PPC is an outbound tactic. However, you usually find paid search engine advertisement as part of a traffic generation campaign for content marketing, which we will talk about now.

Content Marketing

Content marketing is a method of using materials such as white papers, videos, and e-books to both direct traffic to your website in the form of leads and conversions as well as create awareness of your brand. Usually, this content is referred to as "earned media," since it is publicity gained by a method other than advertising.

Usually, this content is developed with the intent of solving the problems of the intended audience by providing information, statistics, resources, or tutorials. Examples are infographics, white papers, and explainer videos. These materials allow brands and individuals to establish themselves as subject matter experts and build credibility with their audience. They will often contain a call to action to drive the audience to make contact with the publisher.

Inbound marketing, when done correctly, can add a tremendous amount of value to your brand, allow you to connect with audiences in an engaging way, and build credibility. Make sure when using inbound marketing that you are measuring your success, setting appropriate goals, and automating the process whenever possible.

Marketing Tools You Can Use

Understanding the types of marketing is an important starting point as you consider what marketing tools to use in your own company. However, thinking primarily in terms of types can be limiting.

For example, here's a list of marketing tools. All of them are effective ways to communicate your message with your target audience and include both offline and online tools. However, notice how many can't be classified as either inbound or outbound:

Tool	Inbound	Outbound	Neutral	Both
Cold calls		X		
Door-to-door sales call		X		
Word of mouth	X			
Referrals			X	
Direct mail		X		
Door hangers		X		
Newspaper inserts		X		
TV commercials		X		
SEO	X			
Social media	X			
Tradeshow presence				X
PPC				X
Public speaking	X			
Social engagement			X	
Flyers		X		
E-mail marketing		X		
Personal letters		X		
Postcards		X		
Radio spots		X		
Billboards		X		
Public relations		X		
Viral marketing		X		
Business directory listings (online and offline)		X		
Website			X	
Books		X		
Webinars	X			

Your own blogs	X			
Landing pages	X			
E-books		X		
Brochures		X		
Guest blog posting on other sites		X		
Catalogs		X		
Client success stories	X			
Your powerful "why" story				X
Free consultation		X		
Lead capture forms	X			
Tidiness			X	
Employee attire			X	
Training staff to be friendly and helpful			X	
Attention to detail			X	
Speed			X	
Flexibility			X	
One-on-one sales calls				X
Calls to action		X		
Limited-time offers		X		
Quantity discounts		X		
Thank-you notes		X		
Overdelivering			X	
Surprise gifts			X	
Unadvertised bonus add-ons			X	
Community groups			X	
Reviews			X	
Social events			X	

Referral programs			X	
Affiliate programs			X	
Letters of recommendation			X	
Coupons		X		
Discounts		X		
Client-only sales		X		
E-mail special offers		X		

If you only think of marketing tools in terms of four categories, many of the tools available to you (like the ones listed above) would never occur to you—primarily those that have to do with building relationships in a more organic way. These kinds of tools may be far more effective for you than whatever is latest and greatest. From a personal perspective, I know sometimes I'd get stuck on using a single tool because I wasn't thinking about all the communication tools I had available. The best marketing tools are the ones you can actually use.

This should be a relief to you. You no longer have to be overwhelmed by the sheer number of marketing tools you "should" or "shouldn't" be using. You're not supposed to use all of them. You only have to focus on the tools you can *already* use or can get someone to help you use.

You no longer have to be overwhelmed by the sheer number of marketing tools you "should" or "shouldn't" be using. You're not supposed to use all of them. You only have to focus on the tools you can *already* use or can get someone to help you use.

For example, our IT services company owner might see "website" on the list of tools above and say, "Well, I don't know how to build a website, but I know a guy who can build a website." He might see "copywriting" on that list and say, "I have a little bit of copy written, but I need more copy written. I remember meeting a copywriting resource at a conference last month—maybe they can write the copy for me." He might see "training staff to be helpful and friendly" on the list and say, "Well, we're already doing that. I never thought of that as marketing."

So when I sit down with my clients, I simply ask them to make a list of all the marketing tools they know they can use. This includes the tools they're already using, the tools they know how to use but aren't using, and the tools a known resource can provide for them.

The cool thing about creating a list of tools like this is that it helps you build your marketing plan faster: it gets ideas out of your head so you don't have to retain them, and it helps you take advantage of tools you already have access to.

In the next chapter, I'm going to show you how to use these tools most effectively by organizing them into a *marketing sequence* based on the customer lifecycle.

Chapter 6

CREATE A
MARKETING SEQUENCE

O kay, we've talked about your marketing goal, your target market, your message, and a list of marketing tools you can use. In this chapter, we're going to begin to systematize everything you've learned so far and put it in the form of a *marketing sequence*.

Earlier I defined marketing as the communication we have with everybody outside our office. However, marketing isn't just a random, hodge-podge set of actions you take whenever you feel like it. The best way to use your marketing tools is within a sequence, where each tool has a clear purpose. Certain tools are used for lead generation, certain tools are used for client nurture, certain tools are used for follow-up, certain tools are used for trying to close a sale, and certain tools are used to keep clients happy after a sale. So when you build a marketing plan, you need to set up a sequence for what marketing activity you're executing at what time, according to the purpose it serves to your clients.

The best way to use your marketing tools is within a sequence, where each tool has a clear purpose.

The Traditional Marketing Funnel

The traditional way to think about sequencing is the concept of the *marketing funnel*. William W. Townsend was the first to associate the funnel model with marketing in his book *Bond Salesmanship* in 1924:

"The salesman should visualize his whole problem of developing the sales steps as the forcing by compression of a broad and general concept of facts through a funnel which produces the specific and favorable consideration of one fact. The process is continually from the general to the specific, and

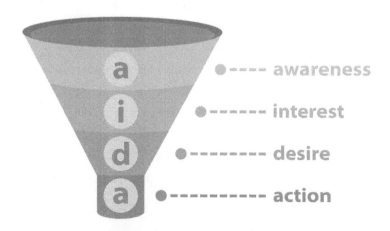

the visualizing of the funnel has helped many salesmen to lead a customer from Attention to Interest, and beyond."[4]

A traditional marketing funnel is often shown with a variety of stages, but the most common representation looks like the image on the previous page.

This is a very simplified version of a sales and marketing funnel, but it is also a common one. It was even referenced in the great sales movie *Glengarry Glen Ross* with Alec Baldwin. In the movie, a company is selling land tracts for homes, and they're not doing so well. So they bring in a sales trainer (played by Alec Baldwin), who is kind of a jerk. He explains that the first prize for the best salesperson is a Lincoln Continental, second prize is a set of steak knives, and third prize is "you're fired". A lot of business owners and salespeople really took that speech to heart, and it's become somewhat famous with the sales and marketing crowd. In that speech, Baldwin's character also goes through this particular version of the marketing funnel: *awareness, interest, desire,* and *action*.

This simple funnel breaks down like this:

- In step one, your prospects become **aware** of your products and services.
- As awareness increases, the prospects' **interest** in your products and services builds.
- As interest builds, you take steps to build the prospects' **desire** for your products and services.

---

4   William W. Townsend, *Bond Salesmanship,* in *Wall Street and the Security Markets* [series], Investment Bankers of America (Arno Press, reprint 1975).

- At the bottom of the funnel, your prospects are ready to take an **action,** such as buying your product or service, or maybe taking another step such as visiting your office or sitting down for a face-to-face meeting.

Notice how as the prospects go down the funnel, the funnel gets smaller. This is because a number of prospects drop off at different stages.

Not every prospect who is aware of your products and services will be interested in it. Not everyone who is interested will build desire for your products and services. Not everyone who desires your product has an immediate need or the available funds to take the appropriate action. Basically, with every stage, you lose prospects—and that, my friends, is the big problem with the above visualization.

This funnel should really look like this:

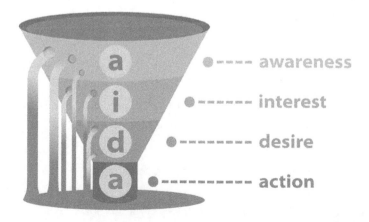

With this visualization, it is really easy to see the huge problem. Your leads are leaking all over the place. As you spend money on marketing to people and get their attention, many are falling out of your funnel, and that's lost time, energy, and money.

The reason there are so many holes is that this four-step funnel model is missing a number of steps in the way people buy. The sales process is actually more complex than this. People want to make their own decisions rather than be told what to buy because information is so readily available in the digital age. Fortunately, there is a much better representation of a sales and marketing cycle. It is called the *customer lifecycle*.

The Customer Lifecycle

The reason I don't like to use funnels to describe the buying cycle is that not only are consumer buying habits more complex but when you think linearly like this you lose out on so much

opportunity. For entrepreneurs like you and I, the customer lifecycle is our "circle of life." Because it reflects the modern client's buying experience more fully, it has seven steps rather than four:

For entrepreneurs, the customer lifecycle is our "circle of life."

Stage One: Awareness

Just like the funnel above, the first stage of the customer lifecycle is building *awareness* about your brand/service. Here is where you work to get the attention of people who don't know who you are or what you do, usually through outbound marketing like newspaper advertisements, pay per click (PPC), webinars, or speaking events.

Stage Two: Knowledge

This second stage is similar to the funnel's Interest stage, but with an important difference. In the past, the prevailing thought behind the Interest stage was to make people curious so they would call for more information. This strategy still works today. However, with the advent of the Internet, people have a greater wealth of knowledge available to them to make better-informed purchasing decisions. Now when people become aware of and interested in a product/service, they want to educate themselves about it. Due to this fact, many modern marketers have taken to "lifting the veil" and providing as much information as possible so the client can have as much knowledge as possible.

So in the Knowledge stage, the prospect begins the journey to learn about your company to see if it is the right fit. This is your chance to establish your company and yourself as the expert and go-to authority on whatever it is you do. Many people feel that the more helpful you are before the sale, the more likely you are to be helpful after the sale.

Here's where inbound marketing works so effectively: landing pages, webinars, live speaking engagements, e-books, newsletters, workshops, teleseminars, testimonials, client manuals, online videos, media interviews, blogs, and in-store conversations can all help educate your prospects and build interest.

Stage Three: Consideration

In the Consideration stage, the prospect has learned about you, researched your product, and put you on a short list of vendors they would consider buying from. Now you have the opportunity to showcase what makes your company and your product or service stand apart from the rest, giving them a small sense of how happy they will be when they choose to engage with you.

Here prospects are going to ask for as much information as they need, so the Consideration stage might go on for a long time. It may go on for months, it may go on for days, or it may take one minute. That's how we buy now. Think about the last time you looked into buying an item. You probably came across a particular person's name in product reviews, and if that person had a YouTube channel, you went and looked at that person's videos about how to use that item in order to get an expert opinion. That's the Knowledge stage. If you were really interested, you did even deeper research on that item, and that's the Consideration stage.

To make the Consideration stage easy for your prospects, offer them as much information as possible in as many different media as possible, such as reviews, more webinars, blog posts, newsletters, and one-on-one sales calls.

Stage Four: Conversion

Conversion is where the deal gets done. All your hard work to help guide your prospect to a purchase has paid off. Just as in the Consideration stage, making a purchase as easy as possible will go a long way to encourage the prospect to choose to buy from you. It will also leave a favorable impression that adds to their decision to recommend you to others down the road. Relevant marketing tools might be a merchant account, acceptance of a wide variety of credit cards, or an online shopping cart.

Stage Five: Fulfillment

Fulfillment is the point where you are no longer educating them about how great your services are, you're proving it. Fulfillment isn't just delivering the product, it's over delivering. It's as simple as doing what you say and going a little further.

Imagine going to a car dealership, paying for the car that you want, and getting a second one for free. Love Chrysler Dodge Jeep dealership in Corpus Christi, Texas, actually does that. Every February 14, they have a buy-one-get-one-free deal, so if you buy a car on Valentine's Day, they will give you a second car for free. That's one example of over delivering on your promise.

On the other hand, when people sign up for my website development service, they're sent a handwritten thank-you note—because for me, that's all it takes to be amazing in my industry. In some highly competitive industries, you need to do more; in others, less.

Over delivering in Fulfillment is where the more unconventional marketing tools come into play: excellent follow-up, attention to detail, generosity, passion, enthusiasm, and eavesdropping on the reviews and comments clients publicize about you.

Stage Six: Advocacy

Over delivering on your promise naturally results in clients who become your advocates. Advocacy means they start talking about you to friends and family, they post reviews for you online through their social media accounts, or they go to review sites and say nice things about you. You can't make advocacy happen, but there are things you can do to assist, such as staying in contact, making sure they're happy with your product or service, rectifying problems in a timely manner, and following up to make sure the problems remain resolved. When you do those kinds of things, clients will naturally start telling other people about you.

Stage Seven: Loyalty

Loyalty is when the client is so happy with what you have done that they continue to buy from you again and again. It results from doing all other steps properly. If you've delivered in all of the areas above, that client is hard to take away from you. Client loyalty is the biggest gift you can get from your client because it means you've done the job right. Plus, getting existing clients to buy from you is way cheaper than finding new ones. To encourage loyalty, you might use reward programs, continued education, and regularly scheduled follow-up.

That's where the line becomes a circle. Loyalty leads you right back to telling your clients about other products and services when they're relevant (Awareness), which leads to them wanting to know more about other products you provide (Interest), and so on. This circle of repeat business can go on and on, as long as you keep up your end.

Creating a Marketing Sequence Using the Customer Lifecycle

The customer lifecycle creates a seven-step sequence, where you can simply plug in your tools at each step. It's an easy, systematic way to get your message out to your target market.

> The customer lifecycle creates a seven-step sequence, where you can simply plug in your tools at each step. It's an easy, systematic way to get your message out to your target market.

Let's return to that long list of marketing tools in chapter 5 and think about the purpose of those tools from the perspective of the customer lifecycle. Some tools are best used to generate awareness, some are best used for fulfillment, and some can be used effectively at multiple stages.

Tool	Use
Cold calls	Awareness
Door-to-door sales calls	Awareness
Word of mouth	Awareness
Referrals	Awareness
Direct mail	Awareness
Door hangers	Awareness
Newspaper inserts	Awareness
TV commercials	Awareness
SEO	Awareness
Social media	Awareness
Tradeshow presence	Awareness
PPC	Awareness
Public speaking	Awareness
Social engagement	Awareness
Flyers	Awareness
E-mail marketing	Awareness
Personal letters	Awareness
Postcards	Awareness
Radio spots	Awareness
Billboards	Awareness
Public relations	Awareness
Viral marketing (such as Dusty Showers)	Awareness
Business directory listings (online and offline)	Awareness

Website	Knowledge
Books	Knowledge
Webinars	Knowledge
Your own blogs	Knowledge
Landing pages	Knowledge
E-books	Knowledge
Brochures	Knowledge
Guest blog posting on other sites	Knowledge
Catalogs	Knowledge
Client success stories	Knowledge
Your powerful "why" story	Knowledge
Free consultation	Knowledge
Lead capture forms	Knowledge
Tidiness	Consideration
Employee attire	Consideration
Training staff to be friendly and helpful	Consideration
Attention to detail	Consideration
Speed	Consideration
Flexibility	Consideration
One-on-one sales calls	Consideration
Lead capture forms	Consideration
Calls to action	Conversion
Limited time offers	Conversion
Quantity discounts	Conversion
Thank-you notes	Fulfillment
Over delivering	Fulfillment

Surprise gifts	Fulfillment
Unadvertised bonus add-ons	Fulfillment
Training staff to be friendly and helpful	Fulfillment
Attention to detail	Fulfillment
Speed	Fulfillment
Community groups	Advocacy
Reviews	Advocacy
Social events	Advocacy
Referral programs	Advocacy
Affiliate programs	Advocacy
Letters of recommendation	Advocacy
Coupons	Loyalty
Discounts	Loyalty
Client-only sales	Loyalty
E-mail special offers	Loyalty

When you have a list of tools you know you can use, and you understand how each tool can fit in the customer lifecycle, now you can start thinking about the types of marketing in a helpful way. It's most effective to use a mix of inbound, outbound, offline, and online tools at each stage. Remember, in chapter 1 you learned that purchase decisions are made subconsciously. In order to get through to the subconscious mind, your message must be seen dozens of times. By tying together online, offline, inbound, and outbound marketing, you have the best shot at getting your audience to take the action you want.

Even if you only use one tool really well for each stage, you can still create an effective marketing sequence that results in loyal clients.

Even if you only use one tool really well for each stage, you can still create an effective marketing sequence that results in loyal clients.

Here's how our IT services company might create its own marketing sequence, with both a simple approach and a multi-touch approach.

A Simple Marketing Sequence

To recap, this IT services company is targeting durable medical equipment companies within a 100-mile radius who have more than five computers and who are concerned about HIPAA compliance. Because it's a relatively new company, its owner John needs to keep costs down, so he starts with a simple marketing sequence. The good news is that the more specific his target market gets, the more success his efforts will have, and the less his marketing will cost.

Step 1: Awareness

John has thought about the tools he knows how to use and the purpose those tools might serve, and he's decided to use postcards as his tool to generate awareness. In order to use postcards, he needs another tool, which his assistant will compile: a mailing list for their target market. Because his target market is so specific, he has only fifty potential leads. Because he also knows that repetition is key to getting his message through, he decides to do a three-postcard campaign, which will really increase his exposure, and which he can afford to do because his mailing list is so targeted.

In terms of his target market's emotional need, John knows his target market is afraid of not protecting their data properly because a breach may mean getting penalized by the government and losing their business. So his target market's deep need is to protect their data at all costs and not have to worry about what happens if their hard drive crashes or their network goes down.

Because John understands how his services meet the emotional needs of his target market, he has a very clear message for his postcards:

Are HIPAA compliance issues
keeping you up at night? We can help!
Visit our website at domain.com/landingpage.

Step 2: Knowledge
If the prospects who received the postcard were interested in learning more about the company's services, they would go to that landing page and find some educational information about HIPAA compliance and the importance of knowing for certain your computers are keeping your patients' data safe.

On that landing page will be a call to action: "If you have more questions about HIPAA compliance, call us to schedule a free risk assessment." A contact form where clients could enter their preferred contact information would follow the call to action.

Step 3: Consideration

When interested prospects get that free assessment and have the results in front of them, they will know exactly what they need to become HIPAA compliant, they will have a clear, targeted product and/or service offering before them, and they will need to decide whether they will purchase it or not. They have now entered the Consideration stage. If the prospect needs more information to make that decision, he or she may ask more specific questions of their contact person at the company to get the information they need.

Step 4: Conversion

In the perfect customer lifecycle world, after the Consideration stage, the prospect would decide to buy. They would place their order and sign their contract. The traditional marketing funnel typically stops here, with the buying decision as the victory. However, as we know from our understanding of the customer lifecycle, John's marketing job is far from over.

Step 5: Fulfillment

Now he and his company have to find ways to overdeliver—to go above and beyond their promise. So when they go to their clients' offices to set up their data protection systems, they also document their entire network and create a complete list of usernames and passwords for everyone who has access to that network that is delivered to the business owner.

Step 6: Advocacy

Like the Consideration and Conversion stage, Advocacy is largely up to the client. To help convert their clients into advocates, John and his company do follow-up phone calls to ask if they are happy with their service and if they have any questions. If they are happy, the company will ask for referrals or make clients aware of other services they provide. Of course, they'll also answer any questions their clients have.

Step 7: Loyalty

To increase the chance that their clients will become loyal clients, John and his company will use the same humble tool of the telephone to do follow-up calls at 15 days, 30 days, and 45 days. During those calls, they will check in with their clients, offer more information on further services, and/or ask for referrals.

As you can see, it's very simple to create a marketing sequence using tools you already know how to use. You just have to remember to flow through these seven steps. Remember, it doesn't have to cost much. For the Awareness stage, 150 postcards are relatively inexpensive. Building a landing page in this day and age is very inexpensive to do—a number of services can help you do it if you need assistance.

The Conversion stage simply comes down having a solid sales practice, so there should be no extra expense there beyond the cost of doing business. In the Fulfillment stage, it shouldn't cost you extra to give people a little more what you told them you'd give them, especially if you properly price your services (but that's a discussion for another time). Advocacy just takes the initiative to follow up. Loyalty primarily takes consistency and time.

Here's a chart summarizing this company's marketing sequence, with its tools listed next to each customer lifecycle stage. Where the primary action needed to be taken by the prospect rather than the company, those actions are also listed for each stage.

Customer Lifecycle Stage	Company Tools and Prospect Actions
Awareness	Postcards Mailing list
Interest	Landing page Response form White paper or e-book
Consideration	*Prospect actions:* Request more information Schedule an appointment
Conversion	Easy-to-understand service packages Credit card acceptance *Prospect action:* Decision to buy!
Fulfillment	Overdelivering on your promises
Advocacy	Follow-up phone calls to ask if they are happy with the product or service
Loyalty	If they are happy, ask for referrals or educate them about other services you provide

A Multi-Touch Marketing Sequence

Let's say John's IT services company use this simple model, he has tested it, and it actually works. They know that a mix of outbound, inbound, offline, and online tools are most effective, and the more touches there are, the more sales they make. So John decides to tweak his plan a bit and adds some more tools to his marketing sequence:

Step One: Awareness

In addition to the three-postcard mailing he did before, John decides to do some cold calls to their mailing list as well, just in case direct mail isn't the best way to reach some of their targets. He also hires a web developer to create a personalized URL to put on the postcard rather than a landing page, so he'll have a record of everyone who clicked on that URL for more information, rather than just for the people who took the time to enter their contact information to sign up for the free assessment.

Step Two: Knowledge

John kept the sign-up form for a free risk assessment on the URL, but he also asked his web developer to add a more open-ended contact form to invite prospects to request more information in general. To help further educate interested prospects, he decided to write a white paper on HIPAA compliance from the durable medical equipment perspective, and when people enter their name and e-mail address, they can download that report for free. He also began a blog (whose link was also on this personalized URL) and posted about ten posts at once to start so there was an archive of information immediately available. Finally, because he and his company had followed up with their clients during the Advocacy and Loyalty stages, he had several good testimonials, so he sent those to his web developer so he could create a testimonial sidebar for the company website (and personalized URLs) as well.

For those who visited the URL but didn't take action, now that they have a record of those people, someone from the company can call them to follow up. This was warm calling rather than cold calling because the prospect has already shown interest. From these calls, the company could get more specific information about why these prospects didn't take action (maybe they weren't really interested, or they needed more information). If information was the issue, the company could help answer their questions right then.

Step Three: Consideration

Consideration happens when the prospects respond positively to these follow-up calls or the original cold calls, or go to their personalized URL from the postcard and take some kind of action, whether it's scheduling a free risk assessment, call or e-mail for more information, download the free report, browse more blog posts, or review the testimonials.

Step Four: Conversion

Just as before, conversion happens when the client decides to buy and signs the contract.

Step Five: Fulfillment

John knew that by promising less and giving more, his company could create a really unique customer experience. So when his clients bought a backup service, as soon as they were done setting up the backup service, his company sent an elaborate thank-you package: a number of branded mouse pads and branded pens, along with a handwritten thank-you note. John made sure he planned ahead and included the cost of this thank-you gift in the sale price, so he wouldn't dampen his enthusiastic customer service with the worry of losing money.

Step Six: Advocacy

John took an additional step to encourage advocacy by arranging to e-mail a client survey, and then following up positive client surveys with requests for testimonials.

Step Seven: Loyalty

Finally, to enhance loyalty among satisfied clients (and advocates), John set up monthly service reviews and quarterly needs assessment meetings. He also hired a writer to create a monthly newsletter and invited clients to opt in. Of course, on every follow-up contact with clients, he made sure they made a request for referrals.

Here's a chart summarizing this multi-touch marketing sequence:

Customer Lifecycle Stage	Customer Tools and Prospect Actions
Awareness	Postcards Mailing list Cold calling
Interest	Personalized URL Response form White paper Blog posts Testimonials
Consideration	*Prospect actions:* Request more information Schedule a free risk assessment Browse more blog posts Respond positively and ask questions during cold calls
Conversion	*Prospect action:* Decision to buy!
Fulfillment	Overdelivery on promises Unexpected thank-you package
Advocacy	Client surveys Follow up positive client surveys with request for testimonials
Loyalty	Monthly service reviews (with request for referrals) Quarterly needs assessment meetings (with request for referrals) Newsletter

Where Most Businesses Struggle: Follow Up

In my experience, most businesses stumble at the two stages of Fulfillment and Advocacy. In Fulfillment, they don't really deliver what they said they would from the client's perspective (much less overdeliver), and in Advocacy, they don't follow up to make sure the client's happy with the product or service. Either way, it all comes down to the failure to follow up.

Most businesses stumble at two stages: Fulfillment and Advocacy. Either way, it all comes down to the failure to follow up.

Following up is one of your most important marketing tools. If you don't follow up with prospects' requests to schedule a risk assessment, then you don't get them to convert. If you don't follow up and deliver what you'd say you'd give them, they're going to want their money back and they're certainly not going to be an advocate for you. Loyalty also goes straight out the window when there's no follow-up. By constantly staying in communication with your clients, you become more than just a vendor. You become a friend and a trusted expert.

Following up is one of your most important marketing tools.

Think about it this way: if somebody comes to your website, fills out a form, and they say, "I am interested in your product," and you don't get back to them for a week, do you still think they're interested in your product? No, absolutely not—you took a week to get back to them. I know following up in a timely manner can be hard. For me, the biggest stumbling block in my business is getting quotes out, because quotes can take a lot of work. That was a failure to follow up. As soon as I created a simple method to create quotes in a timely manner for my prospects, my sales increased.

Let's say I do get a meeting with a prospect: They come to my website, they fill out a form, I do everything they want me to do, and they say, "Yes, I'll meet with you." So I run to their office, I sit down, and I have the meeting. They say, "All right, get a quote back to me," and I take two weeks to get a quote back. It takes a long time to write a quote sometimes. This will most definitely result in a lost sale. I know because I have made this mistake.

So, in order to shorten the time it takes to generate a quote, I purchased a quoting tool that makes it easy for anyone on my staff to create a quote. This allowed my team and me to respond to a quote request in a matter of hours instead of weeks. The end result was more sales because people were impressed with our follow up. Use whatever tools you can to shorten follow-up time, because if you don't respond to a prospect quickly, you are going to lose them.

Here's what a lot of people forget: follow-up is just as important for your existing clients. Once you take the girl to the dance, you should probably call her again, right? So we schedule quarterly lunches for all of our clients. If you're one of my managed service clients and you've got twenty employees, I sit down and figure out what it's going to cost me per head to feed twenty employees, I multiply that by four to get a price for the year, and that number goes into my yearly budget.

The reason I sit down and have a quarterly follow-up meeting with those clients every three months is to ask them, "Where did we fail you? What would you like to see us do more of? Did we get all your problems solved?" What happens after that second or third meeting is that we're no longer talking about what we did wrong. It's just them patting us on the back and talking to us about their families. Now we've built a true relationship, right? I've had my clients call me when my competitors call them and say, "Another company down the street just tried to take me away and I told them No. You come to the company picnics, man. You are part of our team." When you genuinely care about people, money is going to come. When you really want to help people, everything else is going to fall into place—as long as you're genuine.

When you really want to help people, everything else is going to fall into place—as long as you're genuine.

When we send them unexpected thank-you gifts, we also want to make sure we're sending them what they really like. So we send the office manager a note to find out what kind of sports games they like, what kind of booze they like, anything that they enjoy doing to relax– it's as easy as that. You wouldn't believe how cheap you can buy baseball tickets and hockey tickets if you think ahead. Buy a bunch of them and just send them the tickets. I like to send these thank-you gifts out randomly, or just drop by with something in my hand. I do it from a place of honest thankfulness.

For those of you who have an ultra-sensitive manipulation radar, don't worry. The important thing is that I am doing it genuinely. I am not trying to manipulate people. If you're not interested in baseball, and you buy baseball tickets and say,

"Hey, come to the baseball game with me," they are going to see right through it. If you're going to do something with them, make sure you are actually interested in it, too. If you're not interested in it but you know they love it, just give it to them. It might cost you a little bit of money in the short term, but in the long term, it's nothing but profit. So make sure following up is on your list of marketing tools you use in multiple stages.

The marketing tools we have available to us today are virtually limitless. Creating a clear marketing sequence based on the stages of the customer lifecycle will keep you from being overwhelmed by your options and help you use your tools effectively, so you can increase sales and create loyal clients.

Creating a sequence was the final element in our marketing plan. Now it's time to take everything you've learned, and write a marketing plan of your own.

Chapter 7

WRITE YOUR
MARKETING PLAN

O kay, now that you've gotten through the information in chapters 1 through 6, creating your marketing plan is as easy as writing down everything you've learned in an organized format.

Why is it so easy? Let's review all the work you've done so far. In chapter 1, you got rid of your misconceptions about marketing that were keeping you from creating a marketing plan in the first place. In chapter 2, you learned (or were reminded) how to create SMART goals: specific, measurable, actionable, realistic, and time-based. In chapter 3, you learned how to make sure your target market was as specific as possible. In chapter 4, you learned how to create a message that begins with the needs of your target market. In chapter 5, you learned about all the tools of marketing that are available to you, and to focus only on the tools you can use (or contract out) right now. Finally, in chapter 6, you learned how to put your tools in a marketing sequence based on the customer lifecycle, to communicate your message effectively with your target market.

However, because of all the work you've done so far, some of you may be tempted to rush straight to execution, especially if you already have a SMART marketing goal in mind. The problem is looking at the end goal without planning out what it will take to get there can be overwhelming. Think of it this way: Does a builder put the roof on a house before he builds the frame? In that same way, you must fully build the framework before you can cap off your goal with execution. Your marketing plan is that framework is your marketing plan.

The benefit of writing out your full plan in one place is that it makes it much easier to systematically execute it and measure your results (which is the whole point of having a plan, and which we'll talk more about in the next chapter).

Writing out your full plan in one place makes it much easier to systematically execute your plan and measure your results.

So write down your full marketing plan in the exercise below. If you've read the previous chapters, it should take you about 45 minutes. That's right—I over delivered. I gave you 15 minutes of precious time that you can use on the final step, which is to execute your plan.

Exercise 1: Dispel Your Marketing Misconceptions

In chapter 1, did you discover any marketing misconceptions of your own? List each misconception you have about marketing in the form of a statement below, and next to each misconception, list the truth about marketing that counters that misconception. For example:

Misconception: *Marketing is ineffective guesswork.*
Truth: *Marketing is a science that produces measurable results.*

Misconception:
Truth:

Misconception:
Truth:

Misconception:
Truth:

Misconception:
Truth:

Exercise 2: Set Your Marketing Goal

I want you to start by thinking big. Write down one major long-term goal for your business. For example, *In five years, I want to be on the Inc. 100 list.*

Your long-term business goal:

Every long-term goal needs SMART goals to support it. Now write down just one specific, measurable, actionable, realistic, and time-based goal that will support your achievement of your long-term business goal above. This will be your *marketing goal*.

For example: *I will increase sales by 20 percent over the next 6 months by training my customer support staff to offer relevant products and services.*

Your SMART marketing goal:

Exercise 3: Define Your Target Market

1. Name your target market.

2. Who is the buying decision maker?

3. What are your target market's motivators?

4. How far would they (or you) travel to deliver or obtain service?

5. Where would you be most likely to find your target market?

6. Now that you've answered the questions above, define your target market as specifically as you can.

Exercise 4: Create Your Message

1. Start by listing all the *features* of your primary product or service.

2. Now, in a single list, write down all the *benefits* of each of these features that are relevant to the target market you defined in chapter 3. If you're having trouble figuring out what benefits your product or service offers to your target market, consider the following questions:
   - What is the *desired outcome* of your target market, when they're searching for your kind of product?
   - What is the *problem* or obstacle that stops them from having a successful outcome? What gets in the way?
   - How does your product or service help them reach their desired outcome? That answer is the *benefit*.

3. Eliminate any benefit on the list that isn't unique to you. After all, other people can help your target market reach their desired outcome, but what is it about you that sets you apart? What makes your company different from other companies, what makes your service special, what do you offer that your competition doesn't?

4. Then answer the following questions:
   1. What is your most unique benefit?
   2. What problem does it solve?
   3. How does that problem make the client feel?
   4. How will the client feel after the problem is solved?

Now insert your answers in the following blanks to create your USP:

We help __[target market]__ who want ___[1]___ to solve their problem with___[2]__ so they can ____[4]_____.

Your USP:

Exercise 5: List the Marketing Tools You Can Use

Review the types of marketing tools and the list of marketing tools in chapter 5. Now make a list of the tools you know you can use. Include the following:

- Tools you are already using
- Tools you know how to use but haven't started using yet
- Tools you think you know how to use
- Tools you can get someone to help you with

List of marketing tools I can use:

Exercise 6: Create Your Marketing Sequence

Using the list of tools above, fill in each stage of the customer lifecycle below with a couple tools you believe you can use the most effectively and that are best suited for that stage. This will become the sequence of your marketing campaign.

Awareness:

Interest:

Consideration:

Conversion:

Fulfillment:

Advocacy:

Loyalty:

Chapter 8

EXECUTE YOUR
MARKETING PLAN

You finally have a marketing plan and you have all the pieces in place. The only thing that remains is to put it into action. However, don't start making to-do lists or setting deadlines for yourself just yet. Executing the plan is where most people get stuck. Why? Because they think they have to do everything themselves. I'm here to tell that you don't—nor should you.

As an entrepreneur and business owner, you should certainly be the one creating the marketing plan (or at least taking responsibility for getting it done) and making sure the plan gets done, but you really shouldn't be doing most of the tasks yourself. I understand that at the beginning of a new business you may need to bootstrap it for a while, but you shouldn't plan to stay there very long.

As an entrepreneur or small business owner, you
should certainly be the one creating the marketing
plan and making sure the plan gets done, but you
really shouldn't be doing most of the tasks yourself.

In this chapter, I'm going to show you a very simple
approach that will make executing your plan very easy on you.
First, decide what tasks to delegate. Second, create a list of
action steps for each task you're responsible for. Third, create a
marketing calendar to keep everyone accountable. In that order.

Decide What to Delegate

I know, delegating can be really hard for entrepreneurs and
business owners. Who's going to do it as well as you, right?
The fact is no one can do everything themselves—not even
solopreneurs. If you want your business to be around for any
length of time, you're going to have to learn to delegate and
build a team you trust. There's no time like the present.

Since we're dealing with another mindset shift, fight-or-
flight may have kicked in, keeping you from thinking clearly.
So I'm going to make it as simple as possible for you. Here's
what I want you to do:

1. Turn the tools you listed in your marketing sequence
   into tasks or mini-goals.

   Some of you may be insulted I'm mentioning
   this step, but it still needs to be done. Look at your
   list of tools from your marketing sequence and add a
   verb in front of each one, so that you now have a list

of marketing tasks, or mini-goals, that you can either do or easily delegate if you want to. For example, where you might have "website" listed, you'd revise this to "create a website" or "revamp the website," depending on whether you had a website to begin with or not.

2. Decide which marketing mini-goals you should do yourself.

Once you have a list of mini-goals, ask yourself, "Which tasks do I (a) know how to do myself and (b) have time to do myself?" As you're deciding which tasks you have time to do, remember that you need to be reserving ample time in your schedule for working *on* the business and not just *for* the business. Make a list of the mini-goals that you as the business owner should be doing personally and that you're willing and able to take responsibility for.

3. Delegate all the mini-goals you don't have the time or ability to do yourself.

All the mini-goals you can't do yourself, you need to delegate or outsource. If you have a team of employees you can easily delegate tasks to, great. Just make sure they have the expertise to do it well. Most employees in startups and small businesses are overbusy anyway, so for marketing tasks like these, I encourage most people to outsource to a freelancer or independent company that specializes in exactly what you need.

Most employees in startups and small businesses are overbusy anyway, so for marketing tasks like these, I encourage most people to outsource to a freelancer or independent company that specializes in exactly what you need.

For instance, if you have "create website" on your overall list of mini-goals, then you should hire a web developer. If in the process of researching prices you realize you don't have the money to hire a web developer, but you discover you can buy some online website creation software that will be sufficient and that you can use, that's okay. Now you know you need to do it rather than outsource it, and "create website" goes back on your list.

As a business owner, you can't do everything yourself, and you shouldn't. Whatever you do, don't give up too quickly if the first outsourcing option is too expensive. Living in a global Internet economy means you have access to solutions for virtually every budget and timeline, so keep looking until you find a solution that works.

Break Down Your Mini-Goals into Action Steps

Okay, you've decided who is going to do which mini-goal, you've outsourced what you need to outsource, and you have a list of own mini-goals in front of you. Time to dive in and get it done, right?

Unfortunately, it's not that easy. According to behavioral neuroscience professor and *NYT* bestselling author Daniel J. Levitin, executing a multi-step task in sequence, where different tasks with different completion times all need to be finished at the same time, is one of the most difficult things for the human brain to do.[5] You probably already know this from experience, but science is beginning to prove it. He uses cooking and war as examples, but executing a marketing plan is another one.

Because it is so complicated, the key is to keep breaking down your mini-goals until you have a set of action steps that you could do right now if you had to. Levitin agrees: "If you have something big you want to get done, break it up into chunks—meaningful, implementable, doable chunks."[6] (Sounds like a SMART goal, doesn't it?) We talked about the concept of breaking down SMART goals into mini-goals and action steps in chapter 2, but here I'm going to walk you through exactly how to do it with your marketing plan. In fact, executing, in general, is the final step in goal setting, so we're kind of picking up where chapter 2 left off.

Action steps are the literal stepping stones that pave the way to your end goal, help you clearly assess your progress toward meeting your goal, and make execution easy.

Imagine a game of darts. As you make your throws, the dartboard helps you assess how well you did on your turn and how many more points you will need to win the game. Now, imagine playing darts without a dartboard. How will you know if you're winning or not? It might be fun to throw darts

---

5   Daniel J. Levitin, *The Organized Mind: Thinking Straight in the Age of Information Overload* (Dutton Adult, 2014), Kindle location 3233-3262.

6   Ibid., Kindle location 3262.

at the wall, but you won't be moving forward in the game. Or, if you're my friend and client Ben Blaque, you may not even survive the game.

Ben is an amazing crossbow performer who was on *America's Got Talent* a few years ago. He's got a great stunt where he blindfolds himself and uses a crossbow to shoot an apple off his own head. He does it through a series of seven targets facing each other, with each target hooked up to its own crossbow. When Ben hits the first target, that target's crossbow is triggered to shoot an arrow at the second target, which is triggered to hit the third target, and so on, in a zigzag motion, until finally the sixth target is hit, and the sixth crossbow releases its arrow to hit the seventh and final target, which is the apple on his head. If a crossbow hits any target even slightly to the right or the left, that target will spin and the crossbow will miss its target. It may even end up hitting him.

However, even the impossible becomes possible if you break it down far enough into a series of actionable steps. If we stick with the same goal terminology we've been using all along, Ben's big, overarching goal was to use his crossbow performing skills to get recognized on a national stage. He may have listed several mini-goals that would help him reach this big goal, but one of them was certainly to complete his stunt successfully: to hit an apple off his head with his crossbow while blindfolded. So that's his mini-goal.

Even the impossible becomes possible if you break it down far enough into a series of actionable steps.

To execute this mini-goal, Ben needed to break it down even further. His first step was to figure out how he was going to hit that first target, which he couldn't see. He discovered he could use sound: he rings a bell, which helps him pinpoint where that first target is located. His next step was to figure out how that crossbow from the first target was going to hit the second target, and how the second crossbow was going to hit the third target, and so on. Each one of those targets was an additional step toward his overall goal of hitting the apple off his head while blindfolded. He completed each of those steps, so that when he gets on the stage of *America's Got Talent*, he puts the blindfold on, shoots his first arrow, the arrow zigzags across all six targets—tick, tick, tick, tick, tick, tick, BAM—the apple shoots off the top of his head, and the crowd goes wild. That stunt got him on to the semifinals, and he reached his big goal of being recognized on a national stage.

Also, the action steps you choose for each marketing mini-goal must be specific, measurable, actionable, realistic, and time-bound, just like your larger SMART marketing goal. If you have clearly defined how you will know when each smaller goal has been met, it will be much easier to reach your primary goal. In some cases, a well laid-out set of action steps can even be handed to others to complete for you, so you can further use the art of delegation to reach your goal more quickly.

Build Your Marketing Calendar

Once you've delegated your mini-goals and have a clear sense of what you personally need to do (and feel equipped to do it), the next step is to build a marketing calendar. That means setting dates for when each marketing mini-goal needs to be done. Everything needs to be time-based, right? The calendar will help us solidify the timeframe to execute our action steps in order to achieve our goals. So even if you don't have an event on a certain date or another external deadline, you still need to set a timeline of what will get done and when, because your overall goal should have an end date associated with it.

Let's use the example of postcards for our IT company. The owner has decided to hire a graphic designer to do the postcards. He's also decided to hire a developer to set up a landing page. He's going to write the white paper himself.

Keeping in mind his overall marketing goal, which is to get four leads in three months, he knows that his end date for his goal is three months from today. So he needs to start filling the calendar backward from that end date.

Today is March 1. By working backward, he determines that he needs to send out the postcards on March 15. So on his calendar, he puts "mail postcards" on March 15. Now he has to figure out what action steps need to be done in order to mail postcards, and in what order. He knows he needs to create the postcard, compile a mailing list, create the landing page, and write the white paper.

He already has timelines for the tasks he delegated: his graphic designer gave him a timeline of one week to create the postcard, and his web designer gave him a timeline of one week to create the landing page. They can work on that simultaneously, and they're both ready to start today. So he puts "finish postcard" and "finish landing page" on March 8. He's asked his assistant to handle compiling the mailing list, and based on the timeline she's given him, he puts "finish mailing list" on March 8 as well. Because he's delegated those tasks, he doesn't have to worry about anything but the delivery date.

Writing the white paper is his responsibility. He knows the white paper needs to be posted and available the day the postcards are mailed, so he writes "post white paper" on March 15. He also knows he needs to actually finish the white paper a little sooner than that to test the download and fix any glitches before his prospects visit the site. So on March 12, he writes, "Send final white paper to the web developer." He already has a full list of action steps for writing the white paper itself, so he sets a deadline for each one of those action steps, working backward from March 12.

Now that he sees what his deadlines are, he has to decide whether he realistically has time to complete his tasks himself or whether he needs to outsource—even if they are tasks he originally thought he should do himself. People with less money may decide they're going to spend more time getting this done and will still make the time to do it themselves. People with a little bit more money will spend that money on getting these things done quickly. Because the IT business owner has his marketing message so clearly defined and he knows what each one of his mini-goals are, he can easily hand off writing the white paper to a professional writer. If his budget is tight, he might want to offer the writer free services in exchange for the white paper.

Once he has all of his tasks written down with a deadline, and he's assigned them to the people that they need to be assigned to, he needs to make sure everyone sticks to their deadlines. He gives everyone on his marketing team a copy of the marketing plan so that they understand what their part is in the marketing, and to keep them accountable to their deadlines. Then he can focus on meeting his own deadlines, and let the whole machine work together. It will work together, provided he gives it time and revises his goals as needed.

Conclusion:

WHAT'S NEXT?

s I hope you've discovered in the last eight chapters, marketing really isn't that complicated. The most important principles of marketing have been around for a long time, and you had probably heard of most of them—like the importance of selling benefits rather than features, how to set SMART goals, and the customer lifecycle—before you picked up this book. Rather than new principles (or old principles repackaged to look new), what I've found most people need instead is (1) to dispel their misconceptions that keep them from marketing in the first place, (2) a brief tutorial on goal setting so they know what they want their marketing to achieve, and (3) a step-by-step plan that shows them how all the parts work together in a system and helps them take action to get the results they want. That's what I've offered you in this book.

So now that you have a marketing plan, what's next? Once you have a plan, you can delegate a majority of the marketing tasks, track your progress easily, and get on with your other responsibilities as an entrepreneur or small business owner, knowing you've got marketing handled.

The big thing to remember is to simply work the plan and give it time. Don't give up too soon, and don't be afraid to change what you're doing if your original plan didn't give you the results you wanted. Give it time to work, measure the results, and adjust accordingly.

Simply work the plan and give it time. Don't give up too soon, and don't be afraid to change what you're doing if your original plan didn't give you the results you wanted.

I also know a book has its limitations. So if you get stuck at any point in the process, or it doesn't seem to address your particular marketing problem, contact me at http://www. hermanpool.com and I'll be glad to help.

ACKNOWLEDGMENTS

Many people helped me get this book out. Many people helped me form the knowledge I have today. I can't list them all, but know that your lessons and memories are in my heart even if you don't see your name here.

Thanks to:
My Immediate Family: Anita Pool, Kay Clark, Dennis Clark, Marvin Clark, Shenoah Salcedo, Olivia Gonzalez, Oscar Gonzalez, Gerard Solis
(Thanks for supporting and teaching me.)

The A-Team: Brian Freistat, Taylor Swartz, Frank Gurnee, Mersad Buza
(Thanks for building a top-notch team that helps our clients every day.)

David Hancock
(Thanks for putting up with my book delays.)

Margo Toulouse
(Thanks for REALLY putting up with my book delays.)

Every client, employee, and mentor I've ever had.
(You helped me learn along the way.)

ABOUT THE AUTHOR

 Herman William Pool is an award-winning speaker and marketing trainer who has owned and marketed his own companies for over two decades. As founder of Vertical Axion, he uses his experience to help small and medium-sized business owners get noticed and make money through a powerful, easy to follow marketing system. In addition to helping Main Street businesses grow, he has provided his services for Fortune 100 companies.

Herman and his wife Anita reside in Huntsville, Alabama with a few cats and some really nice dogs. He spends much of his free time rebuilding classic arcade machines, finding new ways to help business owners make more money, and hanging out with his grandson William.

A free eBook edition is available with the purchase of this book.

To claim your free eBook edition:

1. Download the Shelfie app.
2. Write your name in upper case in the box.
3. Use the Shelfie app to submit a photo.
4. Download your eBook to any device.

Shelfie

A free eBook edition is available
with the purchase of this print book.

CLEARLY PRINT YOUR NAME ABOVE IN UPPER CASE

Instructions to claim your free eBook edition:
1. Download the Shelfie app for Android or iOS
2. Write your name in **UPPER CASE** above
3. Use the Shelfie app to submit a photo
4. Download your eBook to any device

Print & Digital Together Forever.

Snap a photo

Free eBook

Read anywhere